QUEEN

C. R. JAHN

"My God! Think, think what you are saying. It is too incredible, too monstrous; such things can never be... there must be some explanation, some way out of the terror. Why, man, if such a case were possible, our Earth would be a nightmare."

Arthur Machen, ***The Great God Pan***

Introduction

I present to you a modern classic of occult literature: the strange case of Queenester Pryor. I submit this before the Brethren, the Council, the Grandmasters, and the unaffiliated sages.

By His sign and seal, I do swear that the content herein has been duly investigated, corroborated, and verified. I stand by my word, which is known to you, but anticipate skeptical criticism from the greater community, demanding "proof" of astral phenomena science lacks the instrumentation to detect. This book was not written for the profane.

Of my qualifications, I am permitted to disclose over four decades of occult research, focusing primarily on clairvoyance, projection, and wards. My early studies involved folklore and case reports of manifestations. Influential works included the words of Kardek, Aivanhov, Wickland, Vallee, Seabrook, Reed, and Keel. My studies corroborated much of Queenester's story, which was further verified by the testimony of multiple witnesses, including myself. I have personally observed and interacted with several manifestations which occurred in Queenester's presence, and engaged in further interactions upon the astral. There is no doubt in my mind that she has spoken the truth.

I make no claims of fully understanding this case, and present it solely as an addition to the archives. Perhaps some details may prove useful to another scholar at a future date.

Queenester Pryor is the most powerful witch I've ever encountered, totally feral with no formal training, entwined in symbiosis with one of the Fallen. Her formative years were a nightmare of neglect, abuse, attacks, and homelessness. She is a fighter. Crimes were committed by herself and others. Sometimes people died. This is not an easy tale to read. It is blunt, brutal, and will leave its mark. Reading these words will change you.

At the request of several principals, and under the advice of legal counsel, several events were omitted from the final draft. Names, dates, locations, and other incriminating details were frequently altered for the protection of Queenester and others. In some cases, certain relationships, jobs, and important friendships were given no mention. This was an editorial decision necessary to reduce the length of this book, which became more than twice as long as anticipated.

Queenester does not write books or give presentations like other psychics... she drives a tractor trailer for 5 weeks at a time before returning home for a weekend to swill *Black Magic* rum like a pirate and tear up the dance floor at the goth clubs. She has been a: gang leader, construction worker, mortician, waitress, retail manager, taxi driver, semi-pro wrestler, roller derby referee, stock transfer agent, burlesque dancer, and long haul trucker... now she is my wife.

C. R. JAHN

Dedication

There are too many to thank, most of whom would prefer not to be named. Consequently, this list will be very brief.

First and foremost, I wish to thank my wonderful husband, Clint Jahn, for taking a year off to transcribe and edit this book, and my son Jessey Pryor who gave me a reason to keep moving forward when things were at their darkest.

I humbly dedicate this recounting of my life to: Lucifer, Paimon, Marchosias, Yetarel, Jibril, Anubis, Serpent, Attitude, Gimp, Suze, Mister Meanface, the Animal List, and my Juggalo Family worldwide.

Anyway, as ol' Jack Burton always says, *"Give me your best shot, pal, I can take it."*

Queenester Pryor-Jahn

1

1973, Hof, West Germany

My mother was a whore.

Hanne Lore was a slender woman in her early 20s with reddish brown hair. She loved opiated hashish and fucking. When she discovered she was pregnant with me, she did not know who the father was. She was pretty sure it was a black American soldier, but it also might've been a white American soldier, or a German soldier. Since the black man blew the most loads in her, she assumed it was his. She did not want me. She made arrangements to cross the Czech border and swallow dozens of drug filled condoms to smuggle back to Germany in exchange for an illegal abortion.

Her best friend, Karen, had recently married a black American airman but was unable to have children due to a hysterectomy. She convinced Hanne to give birth with a promise that she would adopt me, and Hanne agreed. How disappointed Karen was when the baby was not half black as anticipated, but she stuck to the agreement. Shortly after I was born, the adoption was formally processed by the West German government and Karen took me home.

Several weeks later, there was a knock at the door. A man in a German Army officer's uniform asked if I was the baby that Hanne Lore had given birth to, and Karen said it was. His face cracked as he held back tears, earnestly begging to hold me, just for a moment, and Karen handed me over. He gently cradled me in my arms for a few minutes, a wide smile lighting up his face as he lovingly gazed down at me... then he handed me back, thanking her, before turning his back and walking out of my life forever. He never told Karen his name.

2

I was ugly, misshapen, deformed... I should probably have been thrown in the trash as my mother intended.

I was born over 2 months prematurely and weighed under two pounds. Karen blamed this on my whore mother's drug abuse. When a baby is newly born, the plates of the skull are free floating, unfused, to facilitate easier passage through the birth canal. It is normal for the crown of the skull to be pressed into a conical shape... with me it was my face, which was transformed into a pointed snout.

I was so tiny I could fit in one of Lafayette's hands. For the first month I was kept in a shoebox. They called me their little "Mousie." That nickname stuck throughout the entire time I lived with them. When I would visit my father's side of the family, the Pryors, I would load up my plate with assorted chesses and they would be all like, "Mousie loves cheese!" A couple times my parents caught me sleepwalking, down in the kitchen, eating cheese.

I still love cheese, especially Brie and Gouda, but don't you dare ever call me "Mousie" or I will punch you in the fucking throat.

3

Karen was a sociopathic control freak... she was also a kleptomaniac... and she took me with her.

Some of my earliest memories involve theft. We would go out to a restaurant and she would always hand me the little lemon scented wet naps that they would provide at barbeque places. "Here, take this, Mousie, in case you need a little wipey later," she would say. Then it would be, "Mousie, put this in your pocket!" Salt and pepper shakers, shakers of red pepper and parmesan cheese, flatware. All of the steak knives we had at home came from restaurants and she never bought spices or condiments. On our way out, she would dump the bowl of complementary mints in her purse.

Once, upon moving to our final destination, she took me to a furniture store, whereupon she bought a full set of furniture for every room: living room, dining room, both bedrooms. There was a beautiful ashtray in the showroom she wanted, but it wasn't for sale. It was made from a large slab of molten lava, with the inside polished smooth... and it must've weighed almost ten pounds. "Mousie... put this under your coat." I always did as she told, and always got away with it.

Many years later, as a teenager, I was caught shoplifting an eyeliner from a store on the 16th Street Mall. Karen was furious when I called her from the police station. "I didn't bring you up like that!" she shrieked. Even though my bail was only $20, Karen decided I should spend the night in jail to "teach me a lesson." I never forgave her for her hypocrisy, and still have flashbacks whenever I smell a lemon handi-wipe...

4

My earliest playmate was a demon.

Shortly after the adoption, Lafayette retired from the Air Force and he and Karen relocated to a townhouse in Aurora, Colorado.

My first memories are of a shadowy figure leaning over my crib, staring down at me. I never saw a face, never saw eyes, just a dark form. I was probably about 2 years old.

The dark figure visited me often. Sometimes I would be awakened by a rhythmic knocking underneath my crib, a deep, somewhat muted tone, like the percussion instrument which is an elongated wooden box with a slit at the top, struck with a rounded xylophone mallet. *Knock, knock, knock...* a distinctive pattern, always the same, almost like a heartbeat or an SOS. I would awaken, terrified and confused, visualizing bowling pins knocking together, but all I could see below my crib were swirling shadows. I would scream for my parents who would assure me that nothing was there, it was only a nightmare, and to go back to sleep. *Knock, knock, knock...* this continued for years. Then, when I was 5, I would feel dozens of hands running over my body whenever I turned on my side. They never touched me when I lay on my back, never grabbed, pinched, or touched me inappropriately, but whenever I turned on my side I would feel the hands moving from my head to my feet.

When I was about 7 I was so accustomed to the shadowy figure I assumed it was my friend and would talk to it. Sometimes it would talk back. We never had deep philosophical conversations because I was fucking seven. We talked about my Barbie dolls and Hot Wheels cars mostly.

Sometimes, I wanted to go outside to play with the neighborhood children, which made the dark figure jealous. "Don't go, stay here with me," it would say. Whenever I came back I would find one of my favorite porcelain figurines broken. It would never smash them, it would simply ruin them by snapping off a piece. It liked to snap the horns off my unicorns. Once, it broke the arms off an antique ballerina over a century old that had belonged to my grandmother, and Karen punished me viciously for that, blaming me.

As I got older, I stopped talking to the shadowy figure and it faded away for the most part, but occasionally continued to make itself known. When I was about 10, my parents would sometimes leave me alone in the house while out running errands. I would be upstairs in my room and hear noises down in the kitchen. Often, the noise sounded like someone had opened the silverware drawer, scooping up a double handful of silverware, then dropping it back in the drawer, over and over again. I would walk down to the kitchen and the noise would stop, and upon opening the drawer everything was found in place. Shortly thereafter, we moved to another house about five miles Northeast, in the predominantly black suburb of Montebello.

One Summer afternoon, I walked to the 7-11 convenience store to pick some things up for my mom and was walking back home when I saw a strange man standing inside an old bus stop which had been out of service for years. He was white, which was unusual in Montebello, and had wavy, sandy brown hair down to his shoulders, wearing a long tan duster and blue jeans. I ignored him and quickly walked past. I was about a hundred feet past him when he shouted out my name. "QUEENESTER!" he said, which shocked me because no-one knew my name... I hated that name and everyone knew me by my middle name, Carol. I turned around. "You're on the right path! You're doing good! Keep going!" he said. Confused, I turned around without a word and kept walking. Five steps later I stopped and turned back around. He was gone. Not just gone, but vanished without a trace. This was impossible... there was absolutely nowhere for him to have gone to... he just disappeared. I was left with a very strong impression that he was an angel.

When I was 11, my parents decided to buy a house a block away. It was at the end of a cul-de-sac and had been vacant for years. A couple of times people had moved in, but they always moved out immediately afterwards. I remember walking past that empty house with my friends sometimes and seeing shadows moving past the windows. It had a foreboding energy that frightened me... it wasn't just haunted, it was a bad place. I begged my parents please not to move in there, but they never listened to anything I had to say.

There was a portal in this house. A huge amount of energy flowed through there. A lot of bad stuff happened after we moved in. Karen's physical and mental health deteriorated rapidly. She would have screaming arguments with Lafayette almost every night, over what seemed like minor insignificant things, or sometimes nothing at all. Montebello was near the scene of the Sand Creek Massacre, and was built atop an Indian burial ground... maybe that had something to do with it, I don't know.

Shortly after I turned 12, the dark figure returned. I would often wake up in the middle of the night to find it standing at the foot of my bed. I was completely paralyzed, unable to speak or move anything other than my eyes. It kept trying to speak to me, telling me not to fight, to listen to what it had to say. It would whisper for hours things I did not understand, about other worlds, spirits, magick... then one day it said, **"You know what you are now. Follow your path,"** and disappeared. The next night three giant dogs materialized in my room. They were only doglike... closer to hyenas crossed with timber wolves. Their eyes were reddish amber but did not glow. They never made a sound, never approached me, and I never touched them. Somehow, I understood they were there to protect me from something, but I must never touch them. They would come and go. Sometimes I would not see them for days. Usually, only one would appear, walking around my bed before laying down and watching me all night. Sometimes there would be two. Occasionally, all three. I called them my Hellhounds. They were bound to that house and never left it, not even to the yard.

Karen took me to a Lutheran church, and I attended the attached Lutheran school. I would talk to the pastors there, asking many questions, but only one would engage me in conversation. He believed I was being visited by a demon which was attempting to attach itself to me and gave me a book to read, advising me, "You just need to have faith."

5

My parents enrolled me in the "Big Brothers & Sisters" program for guidance they were unable or unwilling to provide. My big sister was a lesbian woman who was very nice. She and her girlfriend would occasionally take me skiing, which wasn't really my thing. In the early Spring they took me to the Big Brothers & Sisters annual campout, which took place at a campground which didn't consist of much beyond a lodge house surrounded by small bungalows. Making things worse, there was still nearly a foot of snow on the ground and it was bitter cold. Our days were spent engaged in stupid "team building exercises" in hopes of inspiring trust with the other children, who were boys and girls between 12 and 14.

The second night we were there, about a dozen of us asked the counselors for permission to stay up for a while past lights out in the main lodge building and were told we could as long as we didn't stay up too late, as we "had a big day tomorrow." For some reason, we were allowed to do this unsupervised.

There were about a dozen of us seated in the common area of the huge lodge, on the sofas next to the fireplace. The next room was a large dining area. We sat in front of the fire telling ghost stories. Some of the kids got scared, some got tired, and they began filtering back to the bungalows one by one until there were six of us left, three girls and three boys.

The largest of the kids was an older Mexican boy named Sol. He was nearly 15, heavyset and six foot tall with a military style haircut. Inexplicably, he brought up the topic of demonic possession, which made a lot of the Christian children uncomfortable, myself included. Sol would not drop the subject, fixated on it, insisting that we all join him in discussion. We knew it was a dangerous taboo topic. "We should not be talking about that," I stated.

"What, are you scared?" he mocked.

"Yes, and you should be too. You need to shut up about it. You should talk about something else." A wide grin crossed Sol's face as he continued talking about demons possessing people, taking joy in the fact that he was frightening us... a form of bullying. One of the girls freaked out, screaming and crying, before running out the door to her bungalow. And then there were five.

A smirk crossed Sol's face and he pointed at me. "Holy shit, she's HIM! He's inside her!" Everyone seemed confused. Was he accusing me of being possessed? Was this some sick game he was playing? Disgusted, I got up and walked away too, but instead of returning to my bungalow, I walked through the double doors into the dining hall to be alone. I sat down on the floor with my back to the wall. In the other room I heard a commotion, shouting and arguing... then it went quiet. A few moments later the door swung open and Sol walked in... but it wasn't Sol anymore... his face had completely changed: eyes, chin, ears, cheekbones... his face had narrowed, features becoming sharper, eyes completely black.

He walked over to me and extended his hand. "Come with me if you want to live."

"NO!" Eyes wild, he bared his teeth.

"QUEENESTER! COME WITH ME!" There was no way he could have known my name. Everyone knew me only as Carol, including the counselors. He snatched my wrist, squeezing so hard it hurt, dragging me across the dining hall, towards the kitchen. I was screaming.

Suddenly, the world flipped over as a wave of nausea hit and I realized I was outside my body, looking down on us from the ceiling as I was dragged along the linoleum floor. Then I had a vision... rapidfire images of big sharp chef knives, butcher knives, cleavers... I clearly understood he intended to murder me and began screaming louder, struggling. He pushed open the kitchen door... it was completely dark inside. The other two boys ran into the dining hall and grabbed him, pulling him off me.

The room was spinning, I was too dazed to stand, so I crawled away as fast as I could, still looking down at myself from the ceiling. I made it back to the common room, the girl staring at me wide eyed and pale. I climbed onto the couch and curled up in a ball, weeping, as my perspective snapped back and forth from overhead to back in my body again. I didn't understand what was happening. I felt weak and sick. I squoze my eyes shut until I stopped trembling. When I opened them, I was firmly anchored in my body.

The two boys came back without Sol. They looked shaken, scared. No-one said anything. Then Sol came out. His face was still different, but the other kids didn't seem to notice. He glared at me with raw hatred and pointed his finger. "SHE IS POSSESSED! DON'T LET HER GET AWAY!" he yelled. One of the other boys grabbed a set of deer antlers mounted over the fireplace and pulled them down, holding it like a weapon, with the points facing me. It was a big set of antlers and the points looked sharp. The other boy stood next to him and grabbed them as well. Together, they advanced, as if meaning to pin me to the wall with them. "Don't move!" one of them stammered. Sol smirked.

I don't remember what I said, but told them they were stupid and spent the better part of a half hour talking them down and convincing them I wasn't possessed. Eventually, they hung the antlers back on the wall. I turned to look at Sol and he was sitting on the other couch looking confused... his face was back to normal again. He was crying and claimed not to have any memory of the past two hours, saying "I could see myself dragging you, *but it wasn't me!*"

The next day no-one made eye contact with me, no-one spoke to me, I had no friends.

After the move to Montbello, as one of the few white students I had very few friends, but plenty of bullies. Half the school hated me for the color of my skin, and someone had started a rumor that I was a witch. I have no idea how that rumor got started as I had never told anyone about my experiences and there was absolutely no truth to it. My time at school alternated between isolation and torment.

You know the insult "Your mama dresses you funny?" Well, throughout my entire childhood, Karen insisted on doing ALL my clothes shopping at thrift stores, and I was forced to wear stupid weird ugly shit that went out of style in the 1970s... ill fitting bellbottom highwaters, tan corduroy slacks, sweater vests, penny loafers... I dressed like an autistic spastic and was forced to wear my hair in pigtails. Consequently, I was bullied mercilessly. A mob of blacks would follow me home from school daily, mocking the "white bitch's" stupid clothes. At least once a week they would work themselves up to hitting me a few times, but I was never bashed in the head with a rock or curbstomped, just punched and kicked and told how much they all hated me.

One of the only "friends" I had was a boy named Aaron Will. His mother, Judy (different last name) was a Sergeant with the Denver Police and Karen's best friend, so whenever Judy visited she would bring Aaron along... and we were expected to play quietly while they sat in the living room chatting over coffee. This occurred once or twice monthly, from 3rd grade through 6th.

Aaron was a very strange boy. He was mentally slow, but had some sort of growth hormone disorder. While Sol was unusually large for his age, by the time Aaron had reached 5th grade he was larger than most adult men at about 6'6" and 300#. He was neither fat nor muscular, just large and soft. His father, whom Judy had divorced, was black, and he was a light skinned mulatto with a big afro. In many ways, he reminded me of a golem.

We would be in the basement, playing with my Barbie dolls or Tonka trucks or Lego blocks for hours, and then his eyes, his face, would go completely flat, emotionless, dead, and he would suddenly seize me in a bear hug from behind, or push me up against the wall, or hold me down on the floor. He didn't attempt to touch me inappropriately and never said a word, but would simply hold me motionless for anywhere from 20 minutes to 2 hours, just staring through me with those cold dead fish eyes. This happened almost every time he visited. I could hit, kick, scratch, even bite and he never seemed to feel anything. If I tried to scream he would clamp his giant hand over my mouth and just lay on top of me, a dead weight. Sometimes he would dry hump my leg. I would tell Karen and she would accuse me of lying and beat the shit out of me. Eventually, I learned it was best not to fight or scream or tell on this giant creepy retard and just let him dry hump me until he nutted in his pants. He told me I was his girlfriend. The fact that I repeatedly told him I wasn't didn't matter one bit.

As he got older, he would occasionally try to cop a feel, grabbing at one or both of my breasts, which finally upset me so much I didn't care if Karen punished me. I flat out told her that I did not want to be left alone with Aaron anymore. I would say I didn't want him to come over (as he had begun inviting himself over, without Judy) or that I "didn't feel well" and eventually he got the hint and stopped showing up on his own. Eventually, he stopped coming over with Judy as well, and had been taken out of school. Later I found out that after attacking his younger brother and attempting to burn down his house he was placed in a "special program" for kids with mental problems.

Aaron would disappear for 6 months at a time, then would unexpectedly show up with Judy one day, who announced that he was "doing so much better" since starting some new treatment, and I would believe it and give him another chance as I was expected to do... and he would behave perfectly fine for the next few visits... but then he would start doing the creepy golem thing again, and shortly thereafter would be sent away. This happened at least a half dozen times that I remember. After 6th grade, I did not see or hear much of him for years.

One weekend, near the end of my Freshman year of high school, he came over to hang out. He said that he was on a new medication that made him feel a lot better and had been doing well. He was in brighter spirits and seemed like a completely different person. Karen was in the kitchen and invited him to stay for dinner, and I didn't object because he seemed fine and wasn't acting creepy at all.

While we were watching television, Karen left to go to the grocery store and as soon as the car pulled away he immediately attacked me... no, more than that, he tried to rape me. He got on top of me, holding me down while I fought him, unzipping his jeans and pulling out his stiff cock while hiking up my skirt, struggling to rip off my panties. I grabbed the small Scout knife that Lafayette had given me, unfolding the tiny blade and stabbing him in the leg, right through his pants. The two inch blade sunk all the way to the hilt but he didn't seem to notice... so I twisted it like a corkscrew and began stirring it around while screaming at him to get off me. As suddenly as the attack began, it stopped. He stood up and walked out the door without a word and I never saw him again.

My virtue remained intact, and I was terrified I was going to get in trouble because I just stabbed him and his mother was a cop. I never said a word about what happened to Karen or anyone else.

Many years later, when I was 20 and very briefly visiting Karen for several days after having almost no contact with her for years,

Aaron telephoned the house although there was no possible way he could've known I was there as Karen and Judy had long since lost touch. Karen answered the phone and said it was for me and told me who it was. My blood ran cold. I took the phone.

"What?"

"Hello Queen! It is so good to talk to you! I just wanted to reach out and get back in touch. I am so sorry about my past behaviors and am doing so much better now. I've gotten in a new program with therapy and medication which is working amazingly well! I have a job and my own place now!"

"Wow... I am surprised to hear something finally worked."

"Yeah, well me and my roommates are having a dinner party tonight and it would be so awesome if you could come over and join us! I'd like to introduce you to everyone and we can catch up on old times!"

"I am super busy and don't think I can make it."

"Oh, please?" For old times sake? This would be super important to me! Pretty please? It will be so wonderful to see you! You can bring dessert!" That last thing sounded so discordant I did not think I heard him right.

"Dessert? What would you want me to bring?"

"Just yourself! We want to have YOU for dessert!" he said. I heard other men laughing in the background. Dark, cruel, ugly laughter. I hung up the phone, shocked and repulsed. I felt bile rising in my throat.

I almost want to say that he "hadn't changed at all," but that's not true. He had changed... the Aaron I knew wasn't manipulative, cunning, articulate... he had learned these skills from other predators. Wearing camouflage, using lures, working as a team. He was far more dangerous now.

Aaron Will... remember that name... we are unable to find any data on him anywhere, almost like he dropped off the Earth without a trace... can't find a single record that he ever existed. Decades later, the memory of that telephone conversation still makes my skin crawl.

7

Occasionally, Karen would return to Germany to visit friends and family, and would bring me with her. Usually these visits only lasted a week, but when I was 13 we stayed for 6 months and I was enrolled in a German school.

My grandparents lived in the town of Coburg, which was hundreds of years old and had a castle. It was surrounded by forest. This whole area gave me a profound sense of *déjà vu,* and I intuitively knew my way around the streets of the village as well as the forest paths, as if I had been there before. Walking with my grandparents, I pointed at a figurine shop and stated, "That used to be a clock shop." My grandfather wanted to know how I knew that, but I couldn't tell him. Decades earlier, it used to be a shop where grandfather clocks and cuckoo clocks were repaired.

We visited Hanne for a few days. One night, after dinner, I felt a bit ill and Karen said I had a slight fever and told me to go to bed. I opened the third floor window for the cool breeze and went to sleep. Hours later, a strong gust of wind woke me. I had felt something come into the room with the wind and was frightened. I got out of bed and tried to open the door, but the knob wouldn't turn and the door was jammed shut. I pounded on the door and began shouting for help... and that is when it grabbed me. A long, thin arm wrapped around my chest and pulled, trying to drag me towards the open window. Frantically, I grabbed the doorknob with both hands and screamed.

Karen, Hanne, and Hanne's 13 year old daughter pounded on the other side of the door, also trying to turn the knob and push the door in... then they began trying to kick it in. "Let go of the door! Stand back!" they yelled. The arm let me go and I felt the thing exit through the window. I stepped back, and the door swung open, unimpeded. There was no lock on the door, it did not stick, and it opened and closed with no problems. They told me I had been sleepwalking and was holding the doorknob so tightly they could not get inside. As usual, everything I said was disregarded.

Soon, we returned to America and Montbello. I no longer was visited by the dark figure and hardly saw the Hellhounds anymore.

After the incident with the door, Karen took me to a series of therapists to "find out what was wrong with me," but I was very withdrawn and uncommunicative. Finally, I was taken to a woman whom we were told was very good. She sat me down in a comfortable padded chair and started a metronome... *clack... clack... clack...*

She began asking me a series of generic questions about school in a dull, flat monotone... then started asking about my recent trip to Germany... *clack... clack... clack...*

I remember being told that our time was up, but recall nothing of the session except for a sense of grogginess. There were several more sessions after that, none of which I remembered either. The therapist told my mother that I was prone to flights of fancy, but seemed otherwise normal, and gave her several cassette tapes of our sessions. I later discovered that she was a hypnotist and had been putting me into trance and regressing me. I was never told anything about being hypnotized and never consented to such. Later, we listened to the tapes. It was a lot of boring details about school and my homelife, until she asked about Germany.

"How did you know your way around those streets so well?"

"Because I lived there before..."

"Really? When was that?"

"1788..." She asked for details of my life back then.

"My name was Victoria... I lived with my mother, Marian and my uncle, Joseph... I never knew my father... we lived in a large house with other families... we shared a kitchen... I was 16 years old..." The story continued.

"I met a man named Sidney Lunen at the Marktplatz (central marketplace). He was very nice to me. We began spending time together. He visited my family often. We fell in love... we were to be wed. Then one night, men came to the house while we were sleeping. I awoke to screams. They pulled me from my bed and carried me outside... blood covered the walls and floor... I did not see my mother or uncle. They blindfolded me, bound me hand and foot with rope, and placed me in a cart..."

"I was taken beneath the castle and locked in a room... it was a large room... a nice furnished room with a bed, wardrobe, cabinet, mirrored vanity... there were many fine dresses in the wardrobe, but I was never permitted to leave the room..."

"A man named Devon came to me... he said I belonged to him now... I was expected to do things... I was expected to wear the dresses he selected, eat the food I was brought, smile and behave like a Lady, not try to escape, not to kick at him or his servants or throw things at them... I was expected to comply. Devon had lights in his eyes that would turn to flames when he was angry. When he was angry he would glare at me and it felt like I was on fire, burning from the inside out..."

"I refused to eat and screamed every day until Devon brought Sidney to my cell. He stood outside the barred window with a dagger to his throat, threatening to cut his throat to the bone if I continued to refuse his demands. 'Please, do whatever he asks of you!' Sidney begged. I began to comply. Devon gloated about how he finally found me and I would never leave him again... but I had never seen him before..."

"Days later, I began exploring the cell... in the drawer under the vanity I found a letter opener... I slid the point under my chest and slammed myself against the wooden cabinet... it went through my heart and I died."

I remembered nothing of these sessions, but upon listening to this tape a flood of much older memories started coming back... not just from the 1780s... centuries earlier... millennia... I certainly knew Devon before, in several past lives... Sidney too... but they had different names then... different forms... they were not human, and neither was I. It took years, decades, before I finally was able to put all the pieces together.

The therapist thought my story showed I was very creative and had a good imagination. Karen saw that as incontrovertible proof that I was a liar and troublemaker. The "fantasies" I had of being engaged to Sidney and raped by Devon in a past life were interpreted by my mother as an admission that I had been engaging in premarital sex. She began calling me a "whore like your mother" and accused me of being on drugs. I was a virgin and didn't even smoke cigarettes.

I noticed a profound change in Karen around this time. Her eyes became wild, like a feral animal. She showed her teeth. She was constantly angry, negative, crazed, lashing out. She became nasty, hateful, finding fault with everything. She screamed at myself and my father daily, over nothing at all. She began beating me with a heavy wooden spoon, breaking several. Sometimes she used a clotheshanger. If I cried, she beat me harder. If I begged her to stop, she would slap me across the face for "talking back." If I put up my hand to block whatever she was beating me with, I was accused of "fighting back" and would be beat until her arms were tired. I was always covered in bruises and welts. I was living in Hell.

8

Eventually, Karen returned to Germany for about a year, and it was as if a crushing weight had been lifted. Her control over me was no more. I had been liberated!

As soon as I turned 15, I got my Learner's Permit and was allowed to take our blue Cavalier for short rides to the grocery store and back. Eventually, I realized that Lafayette either didn't notice or didn't care if I was gone for a few hours, as long as I returned at a reasonable hour. If I had decided to stay out all night he would have taken my driving privileges away, but a few hours in the afternoon or early evening was fine. I would make up any excuse to go for a drive, and eventually got a job at McDonalds, to which I was allowed to drive back and forth. I only worked part time, but told Lafayette I "needed the car for work" on my days off as well. This was never questioned.

One day, while out for a drive, I felt a compulsion to turn onto Colfax Boulevard and keep driving East. After a few twists and turns, I discovered Eastlawn Cemetery. Back in 1988 it was still undeveloped with no buildings or spotlights, surrounded by desolate wastelands on every side. I loved walking amongst the ancient tombstones. This became my sanctuary, to which I returned every chance I got, at least twice a week.

There was an old man in our neighborhood who sold beer and cigarettes to the high school students, but the brands he stocked were very limited, so that is how I began drinking Mickey's Big Mouth malt liquor and smoking Marlboro reds. I would hang out at Eastlawn for hours, with a beer in one hand and a cigarette in the other, to relax and be alone with my thoughts.

Sometimes I would have conversations with the birds, whistling to them, mimicking their calls. They would cock their heads at me and whistle back. Occasionally, one would even fly down and perch atop a tombstone near me and we would whistle back and forth.

I would talk to the spirits here too. I never had anything really Significant happen, although I mostly visited during daylight hours, but sometimes I would hear a voice talking in my head, always a different voice, seldom got their name, saying silly stuff mostly, stuff I didn't always understand. Sometimes I would talk back and occasionally they'd reply, but we never really had any actual conversations, and frankly I half assumed it was a figment of my overactive imagination. It didn't matter. As far as I was concerned it was a relaxing way to entertain myself far away from everyone else. This was my happy place...

9

Karen did not like that I had been goofing off and skipping school because Montebello was horrible. She schemed with a friend of hers to get me enrolled at Thomas Jefferson High in the prestigious lily white community of Cherry Creek by getting mail delivered to her friend's house as "proof" we resided there.

I needed to wake up at 0430 every morning to take the first of three buses to get to school every day. I always arrived 45 minutes before the teachers did, with no-one there except the janitors. I would go to my locker, punch it for 15 minutes, then sit down and play my guitar until classes started.

I didn't know anyone there, but was able to enroll in a guitar class which I enjoyed. One of the only black kids in the school was in my class. He hated everyone. I said "Hello" to him and he literally snarled. I thought that was adorable and made a point to say "Hello" to him every day. He would try really hard not to smile. His name was Tony, and sometimes while we were supposed to be practicing Flamenco we would play Metallica on our school issued nylon stringed acoustics instead, to the delight of the other students.

I eventually began hanging out with the metalheads at my new high school. Sometimes we would go for drives in the barren wastelands East of Denver, exploring the unpaved backroads while listening to music, drinking beer, smoking weed...

We would drive up and down the infamous Picadilly Road, which the high school kids called the "Highway to Hell" based on all the urban legends: haunted 3 Mile Bridge, the Albino Man, and rumors of Satanic cults conducting human sacrifices...

One night, we saw fresh tire tracks going deep into a field of tall grass, so I told my friends to follow them. The tracks branched off several times in different directions, but my intuition kept pulling me along a very specific path which I instructed the driver to follow. Soon, we saw the glow of a fire as we climbed a rise. We cut the lights and pulled over, very quietly exiting the car, walking further up the trail until we got to the top of the hill, where we saw a van and a half dozen cars parked in the field and a bonfire in the distance. We cautiously approached, using a row of hedges to conceal our movement.

There was a group of people, all wearing red robes, performing a ritual in the light of the fire. The field was all dirt and dead grass, except for where they were standing... a large circle of black dirt with a small tree at the center. There was no black earth of that type visible anywhere else, and the tree was dead, sun bleached, twin branches stretching towards the sky... bloodstained nails were sunk into each branch from where sacrifices had been crucified. A girl hung there, but she wasn't nailed to the branches, ropes tied her hands to the nails. Her head hung down as if she was drugged or unconscious... she was nude, with long brown hair and the undeveloped body of a 13 year old.

All of the cultists had their hoods up except for one, the leader. He had slicked back black hair and the stereotypical villainous goatee, but also prescription glasses and a lazy eye that likely resulted in him being relentlessly teased as a child. Perhaps that is why he chose to lead an evil cult? He held a dagger in his hand which he would gesture with intermittently.

He spoke words in a language I did not recognize... it was not Latin or Spanish anyway. He would speak, and then a dozen cultists would chant in unison, also in that strange language but different words. This continued for quite some time, growing louder, more urgent. We were terrified. Was he actually going to sacrifice this girl in front of us? Then he turned and locked eyes with me... but it was impossible for him to have seen us, hidden motionless behind the bushes as we were.

Silently, we crawled away from the bush, back over the rise, and ran like a motherfucker back to the car. We gave no fucks about making noise at this point, slamming doors and peeling out as we drove back along that trail as fast as we could, luckily not wrecking or taking any wrong turns. No-one chased after us.

We talked about it a couple times after that, but soon my new friends became distant and we eventually drifted apart and never hung out again. I don't even remember their names.

10

Eventually, school administration somehow discovered I did not reside in Cherry Creek so I was forced to return to Montebello High. My Junior year started out as complete shit, because the teachers working there didn't even measure up to the level of negligent incompetence.

Sayeed was a huge black man who supposedly taught American History... he was also the football coach. He never bothered to teach us anything at all. He would say, "Read pages 22 to 28 in your textbook," and that would be it. While he sat at his desk, the football players would approach to have brief conversations and purchase steroids and amphetamines. Other students would purchase eighths of weed or tiny quarter gram baggies of coke. Everyone knew about it. It amazed me that he didn't get busted until years later. Our 'roided and tweaked ghetto football team was undefeated so a blind eye was turned to his drug dealing for a long time.

Our Economics teacher was near retirement age, an old white guy with white hair and thick Coke bottle glasses who was fond of sweater vests and screaming. He never taught us anything either, but instead would lecture endlessly on topics like, "You kids today," and "This generation has no respect." The most bizarre thing about this was that the students in the class were generally very well behaved. That did not seem to matter at all. From day one he had decided that we all had the wrong attitude and needed to learn to mind our elders. This was all he talked about, throughout the entire class, every single day. The students would get so exasperated they would literally beg him to please open the textbook and teach them about Economics, whereupon he would point to them and screech, "THAT IS EXACTLY WHAT I MEAN! NO RESPECT!"

I also was forced to share a locker with a crazy Christian girl who tore up the Ozzy poster I taped up inside the locker door, then would tear up my notebooks, my homework papers, throw my coat in the trash, leaving notes calling me a "Satanic whore" and threatening to beat my ass. One day she confronted me, backed up with three other girls, all bigger than her. They were following me down the hall and she was yelling, "HEY! DEVIL GIRL!" while her fat friends snickered. I turned around. "WHERE ARE YOUR DEMONS NOW, BITCH?" she yelled, clenching her fists like she was about to take a swing.

I felt something shift inside me, changing my face as I grinned sharply and said, "They're EVERYWHERE." Her eyes got wide and she gasped, seeing something she did not expect, and her friends immediately scattered. No-one bothered me again after that.

I soon decided that Monteghetto High was a total waste of my time and dropped out to pursue a rewarding career opportunity in the fast food industry.

I needed to take three buses to get to and from the Burger King at Chambers and Illif, just like when I attended Thomas Jefferson High, which was a huge pain in the ass that wasted hours of my day. When my co-worker, we'll call her "Becky," announced she needed a roommate to share expenses, I told her I'd move in because that meant taking only one bus to work without any transfers.

Karen and Lafayette both sort of pretended to act like concerned parents when I ditched school and stated I was moving out, but when I told them I would simply apply for "emancipated minor" status, they quickly shut up and even helped me move.

Becky was a basic bitch from a rather affluent family who had dropped out of school at 17 and her parents paid her bills but did not give her an allowance because they wanted her to "learn responsibility" by working at a job... hence her prestigious position as a Burger King cashier. Her friends were all privileged yuppie preps. Often she would invite them over to drink Michelob and *Stolichnya* and listen to shitty 80s pop music with the creepy fat 30 something alcoholic neighbor who would buy the teenagers booze in exchange for being allowed to hang out.

I never really fit in with Becky or her friends. I would hang out at their gatherings and drink a few beers, but I wasn't really into their music or small talk and didn't dress like them either. I preferred *The Cure, Guns & Roses, Ozzy*, and I wore all black with dark purple lipstick and thick black eyeliner... I also read tarot cards.

As far as I knew they never saw the small altar hidden in my closet, but had decided I was a "witch" anyway.

After I had been living there about 4 months, Becky asked if I wanted to go out to the movies with them. It was the first time they had ever asked if I wanted to be included in any of their activities outside the apartment, and I was happy to accept. We piled into two cars and drove out East, past the cinemas, beyond Chambers, out of Aurora. "Where are we going? There's no theaters out here?" I asked.

"Oh, don't worry... we just need to make a quick stop first. They pulled into Eastlawn Cemetery, my secret sanctuary, but something felt horribly wrong. I could feel a panic attack coming on.

"Why are we stopping here?"

"Oh, we're just going to hang out a bit before the movie starts," Becky said. Something rang false in her tone. I knew she was lying to me. She and her friends had planned something. We parked and everyone got out of the cars, there were 10 of us altogether. The person driving the other car popped his trunk and took out a shopping bag, reaching inside and handing out candles to everyone... everyone except me. They were generic white tapers like they sell at the grocery store.

For a few minutes the preps whispered amongst themselves as they attempted to light their candles, but the crosswind would blow them right out. Soon, they gave up and handed them back to the boy who returned them to his trunk. They began splitting up into small groups, wandering around the graveyard by the light of the full moon. No-one seemed to have brought any beer or weed, and I don't even think they ever said what movie we were supposed to have been going to. It seemed like they had formulated some half-assed plan to bully the witch, then something happened to confuddle them, whereupon they began aimlessly walking around, waiting for someone to tell them what to do.

"QUEENESTER!!!" a booming voice spoke out, seemingly from all directions or directly above us. Everyone froze. This must've been the prank they'd been planning to scare me.

"Very funny... where are the speakers?" I asked. Then I remembered that none of them knew my name... everyone called me by my middle name, Carol.

"QUEENESTER!!!" the voice boomed again, like thunder. All the preps looked confused and scared. I didn't see any wires, speakers, or evidence of a PA system hidden in the bushes. It certainly wasn't a bullhorn.

"QUEENESTER!!!" Thick fog suddenly appeared out of nowhere, rapidly rolling over the highway and across the graveyard. It was so thick we could not see someone standing 10 feet away... I could hear some of the preps crying out fearfully... then it slowly began to fade. Over a hundred shadowy figures stood, shoulder to shoulder, around the perimeter of the cemetery.

The figures were not clearly distinct, but were all different from each other, like the Goetic entities that were part animal and part man. Some appeared like men in robes, armor, costume... many wore crowns. They did not speak and did not approach, but they were not still like statues either... I could see them shifting their shoulders, tilting their heads, expressions on a few bestial faces. They were all taller than men, but not giants... maybe about 9 feet tall, encircling us, perhaps a 50 feet radius from where I stood. And then they were gone, as the fog dissolved into wisps and vanished.

All the preps were shaken and pale. No-one spoke. We all returned to the cars and drove back to Aurora in silence. We never saw the movie.

12

After the manifestation at Eastlawn we stopped at a convenience store to get a 12 pack before pulling up to Becky's friend's house, behind the other car. We went inside, walking into total chaos.

"As we were driving back, Kelli started freaking out! She was screaming and hurting herself!"

"She's on the bathroom floor having some kind of fit! Something is really wrong with her!"

"One of those things got inside of her! She's fucking possessed!"

"It's all HER fault! The witch! They were saying HER name!"

"You need to DO SOMETHING about this, witch! You need to FIX this!"

They all glared accusingly at me. It was not my idea to go to Eastlawn... that was totally on them, and they had obviously been up to no good. They probably had planned to grab me and ritualistically torture me as some sort of depraved team building exercise... unless I was in abject peril I can think of no other reason for such a dramatic manifestation. Who is punked now, motherfuckers? But regardless, they were all really scared and pissed off and had no intention of letting me leave. I shrugged and followed them to the bathroom.

The prep girl they called Kelli lay on the linoleum floor, convulsing, covered in vomit, emitting feral growls interspersed with the occasional shriek. It was a real shitshow and she probably needed some Thorazine.

"You need to FIX what you did to her, witch!"

"YOU did this! This is all YOUR fault!"

"You need to get it out of her!" I stared at them. Their eyes were wild. They looked like they intended to lynch me.

"I didn't do anything to her. I don't know how to help her."

"Can't you, like, do an *exorcism* or something?"

"I've never done one before, but I suppose I could try. We can't do it here though."

"Why the hell not?" The boy looked enraged, like he wanted to hit me.

"Whatever got into her came from back there... so we need to go back there to put it back where it belongs," I explained, as if I knew what I was doing. I had no idea what to do, those words just came out, but they seemed to make sense. They frowned and talked amongst themselves, obviously upset about the prospect of returning to that place, but eventually they agreed and carried her back to the car.

We piled into the other car, but as soon as we approached Tower and Smith Road I had a strong compulsion to go Northeast... I directed the driver towards Picadilly and 56th... towards the Satanic sacrifice spot. He didn't argue and the other car followed.

I directed them to carry her to the dead two-armed tree.

"What is this place?"

"Why is that tree all by itself? Why is the dirt all black?"

"Why are there nails in the tree? *Is that blood?*" I shook my head at these ignorant fucking monkeys.

"Just lay her down at the foot of the tree. Whatever is inside her came from this portal, and I need to send it back where it belongs."

They laid her down where I asked. I had no fucking idea what to do, so just went with my gut and decided to wing it. She was unconscious and still... I gently rolled her onto her side, placing one of my hands on her brow, the other on her back between her shoulder blades and, for want of a better word, began praying.

I'd denounced Christianity years earlier because the Lutheran pastors were unable to answer my questions, telling me I "just need to have faith." Faith in a "jealous" God, a wrathful God who inflicted pestilence, floods, war, famine... a dysfunctional abusive bully who demanded fear in exchange for love, threatening an eternity of torture in Hell simply for failing to swear allegiance to Him. So I certainly couldn't call upon Jesus or Michael or St Benedict.

I decided to call upon my invisible friend, David, who I met years earlier via a type of playing card divination similar to *Ouija* in which cards represented letters and could spell words. The name "David" kept being spelled repeatedly over the years when I asked whom I was speaking to. He always seemed to be around, and he'd never played tricks on me or was mean. He seemed to be more of a companion than a guardian or mentor, but I couldn't think of anyone else to call.

"David, I need your help!" I whispered. "This girl was possessed by an evil spirit and I need to get it out! I am so afraid of what these people will do to me if I fail! They accuse me of causing this, but I didn't do anything! Please do whatever you can, call whoever you can, to get this spirit out of her!"

I do not know if David responded to my pleas, but as I sat under that tree where so many people had been ritualistically sacrificed, *something* certainly heard me... suddenly, *I* was possessed too! I felt this powerful energy flow into me as my focus narrowed to tunnel vision on the girl's face and a flood of words I didn't understand poured from my lips. I was speaking in tongues, glossolia they call it, for the first time in my life. I had absolutely no idea what I was saying... something else was speaking through me.

I felt lightheaded, detached, as if I was watching myself through someone else's eyes. Suddenly, she shuddered and a mist was expelled from her mouth, whereupon she immediately relaxed. In my mind's eye I had a vision of a humanoid face: pale, rawboned, greasy, with an impossibly wide toothy grin. I envisioned it exiting her and sinking deep beneath the jet black soil.

The energy within me departed and my perspective was restored. The girl's eyes fluttered and she coughed loudly, twice, before asking where she was in slurred words. She seemed hungover, but had been sober earlier and no-one had been drinking. Her friends helped her back to their car and presumably took her back home. The driver of the other car dropped myself and Becky off at our apartment. No-one thanked me. No-one said a word to me. Everyone seemed angry, resentful, sullen. It was an ugly hateful vibe. For the first time in my life people seemed afraid of me.

My relationship with Becky immediately soured. She avoided eye contact with me and spoke in sharp clipped tones. Although she never said it, it became clear I was no longer welcome there.

A few days later she held another get together at the apartment with her friends and the creepy fat guy who bought them booze. The vibe was cold and hostile so I retreated to my room, closing the door then going into my walk-in closet to sit before my small makeshift altar to meditate, clear my head, wish myself far away...

I am not sure how much time passed, but suddenly I snapped back to my body to find myself violated. The creepy fat guy had gotten shitfaced drunk, intruded into my room, stumbled into my closet and collapsed on top of me, pawing and groping at my breasts as he disgustingly licked and slobbered all over my neck. I screamed and punched him until he rolled off me so I could escape, running out into the living room to tell Becky what he had done.

She laughed. They all laughed like they thought a 15 year old virgin being molested by a thirty-something alcoholic was hilarious. In retrospect, they had probably dared him to do it to get back at me in some way. I returned to my room as creepy fat guy was stumbling out and kicked him in the balls. He took a few more steps and toppled over, whether from the kick or the drink I don't know. I picked up the phone and called my friend Gizmo who said I could crash on her couch for the weekend. I packed a small bag and walked out without a word. No-one asked where I was going, they were just glad I was gone.

14

When I returned to the apartment on Monday there was a new doorknob on my bedroom door which required a key. Even though I was paying rent and had been added to the lease (which required Lafayette to co-sign), that bitch Becky had locked me out of my own room! Fortunately, she was rather stupid and it wasn't a very good lock... simply shimming the latch with my laminated driver's license popped it right open.

I didn't own much, but what little I had was destroyed. I used to collect Breyer horses, which were my most prized possession. One of Becky's friends also collected them, and apparently decided to steal over a dozen of mine, choosing the valuable, rare, out of production ones and a few others she fancied. Other figurines I owned had been contemptuously smashed, then placed back on their shelves to mock me. All my best clothes had been stolen, leaving me with nothing but T-shirts and my Burger King uniforms. All of my drawers had been ransacked and dumped on the floor, even my mattress had been pulled off the bed.

Devastated, I bagged up what few things of value I had left and called Lafayette. He drove from Montebello down to Centennial with a truck to load my furniture into so I could move back home. I left the Burger King uniforms hanging in the closet and never saw or heard from Becky again.

15

Karen had moved back from Germany and was more horrible than ever before. She blamed me for everything. She tried to control my every move, like I was in a prison, and had confiscated my wallet with the identification documents I needed to get a new job. She screamed at me constantly, slapping me across the face, beating me with a belt, throwing things at me from across the room, for reasons that made no sense, or for no reason at all. And of course I was no longer allowed to drive the Cavalier.

After only three days of this, I resolved that I would rather die than spend another moment in that wretched house subjected to constant abuse by that insane creature, and walked out the door with nothing but the clothes on my back and two quarters for bus fare Downtown.

My friend Gizmo let me crash on her couch for a week, but told me that her landlord required that I be added to the lease and I would need to pay towards rent as well... but that was not an option as Karen had taken and hidden my learner's permit, alien card, Social Security card, even my birth certificate, so employment was not an option. At the end of the week I was homeless on the streets of Denver.

16

There was a coffee shop called *Muddy's* at 22nd and Champa that
most of the street kids hung out at because it was one of the few
places we weren't run out of. It was owned by the Blues musician
Muddy Waters, and they played instrumental Jazz all day, which I
hated, but at least it wasn't Country. They were open from 4 PM
to 4 AM and sold a mug of "bottomless coffee" for a buck fifty,
which was a mix of Columbian and espresso with unlimited self-
serve refills. They had a small reading library upstairs with books
for sale and occasionally would have live bands. It was the closest
thing I had to home while I was on the streets.

I would panhandle for change on the 16th Street Mall until I could
afford a mug of coffee and a plate of nachos, or if I was feeling
extravagant their "Shameless Pizza," which was a bagel with cream
cheese, tomato, olives, pepperoni, and mozzarella cheese toasted
in the oven. On rainy days I sometimes couldn't get any money at
all, so when a customer got up to leave I would snag their mug,
rinse it out in the bathroom sink, and have free coffee until they
closed. I was there every single day, usually from 4 to 4, and
would walk to Tom's Diner after that to have another cup of
coffee if I had money... otherwise, I would just keep walking all
night. Sleep deprivation was like a drug, making me groggy,
forgetful, careless.

A few days later, I walked into the Woolworths on the 16th Street
Mall, conspicuous in my grungy stained clothes, oblivious to the
loss prevention agents shadowing me, as I shoplifted a single $1.29
eyeliner and walked out the store, whereupon I was immediately
apprehended.

Woolworths had a zero tolerance policy and had the Denver Police arrest me and take me to jail. I was laughing and joking with the female cop, and she remarked, "You should think about being a cop... you're good under pressure," just before dropping me off at the police station for processing. I was placed in a holding cell and they called Karen.

When she arrived, I could hear her loud booming voice from around the corner. "I do not know what is wrong with her, I certainly never taught her to do this, she is simply unmanageable and perhaps a night in jail will teach her a lesson!" And then she left.

She never taught me? *"Mousie, put this in your pocket."* Right. Afterwards, a policeman came to my cell and told me that, as a minor, they were required to release me to the custody of a guardian, but if I did not want to go home with my mother they could contact Social Services to find me a foster family. I thought about that for exactly 5 seconds. That would require a lot of paperwork and bureaucratic bullshit, after which I would be thrown into the system with no idea to whom I'd be assigned. I had heard stories about farmers becoming foster parents to get paid by the state for each slave laborer they fed and housed, and of course other stories about the freaks who liked to molest kids. I shook my head and said I wanted no part of that, I'd just go home with Karen. "The Devil you know is better than the Devil you don't."

17

Karen picked me up the next morning and, once we got in the car, informed me that "There are going to be a lot of changes," before screaming about what a piece of shit I was, a whore and drug addict just like my worthless mother. I was still a virgin and did not use drugs, but she would not believe anything I had to say.

When we got to the house, she told me that I needed to live by her rules and would need to work at a job she chose and pay rent every week. She also had locked the security bars for all the windows and doors so I remained trapped inside without a key. And then, for good measure, she beat me with the belt again just to remind me who was boss.

After she drove away, I discovered that one of the second floor windows to her bedroom had the bars unlocked, so I was able to climb out on the roof. The problem was my boots were locked in the garage because we were not allowed to wear shoes in the house... and I had no money for bus fare and was ten miles from Downtown.

Karen had a large water dispenser bottle filled with years worth of pocket change, and I was able to shake out about twenty bucks worth of quarters I filled up the pockets of my denim jacket with. Then I grabbed two wire clothes hangers, unwrapped them, straightening and connecting them, fashioning them into a long hooklike tool.

I jumped down to the ground and walked to the side door of the garage. The bars covering the door were locked, but the door itself was not. Opening the door, I tried repeatedly to snag my boots, whistling the "Mission Impossible" theme the whole while. Eventually, I snagged them both, pulled them on, and trudged to the bus stop. I vowed never to return, never to be under the shadow of that house again. I was free.

18

ZAN.

I am "Zan" now.

That was my new identity, with my dark purple lipstick, spiked New Wave hair, and the black leather boots with silver toe and heel caps Lafayette had given me for Christmas. I had different colored bandannas tied around my ankles and wrists too. I liked my new look.

When you are on the streets, no-one uses their given legal name. Many reasons for this. First of all, we were committing crimes. At that time, vagrancy and panhandling were still illegal, and of course petty theft, trespassing, fighting, stealing from one another, drugs, weapons, whatever. Whenever someone got arrested, they might try to get off by ratting out everyone they knew... but if they did not have your Name that information could not be entered into the system and was a lot less valuable. Many of us had active warrants, usually for Failure To Appear on some bullshit minor charge. Some of us had people looking for us like abusive parents. And, of course, nearly everyone was a piece of shit, some a lot worse than others, and the last thing you needed was a crazed stalker finding out your Name.

Karen came down to the 16th Street Mall a few times, showing people my high school photo and calling me "Queenester." People told me she'd been around several times. She even showed up at *Muddy's* once while I was on the smoking patio. Everyone knew I was there, but no-one told her shit. "Snitches get stitches" actually meant something back then.

I enjoyed hanging out at *Muddy's*. Many famous, and soon to be famous people hung out there: Rosanne Barr, Trent Reznor from *NIN*, Ogre from *Skinny Puppy*, and Jhonen Vasquez creator of "Johnny the Homicidal Maniac" were all regulars.

Hunter S Thompson briefly haunted *Muddy's* as well, when Hell's Angels leader Sonny Barger was a fugitive hiding from the feds and he was helping him. Sonny had disguised himself by bleaching his hair blonde and wearing a Hawaiian shirt, cargo shorts, and sandals... he hung out with my biker friends Gimp, Eyeball, and Gumby. They were so secretive about it I did not find out who he was until 30 years later.

There was a very heavy spiritual vibe amongst the diverse patrons, which included celebrities, authors, musicians, college students, and homeless street kids. I had deep conversations with college professors and astronomers about Quantum Physics, wormholes, and dark matter before they became mainstream topics, somehow having a working knowledge of topics I'd never studied, and they could not fathom how I could possibly know so much about these things. I had no idea either, I'd always known it, ever since I was a small child. I spent a lot of time drinking strong coffee and playing chess. I look back on these days as one of the best times of my life.

Before *Muddy's* opened at 4 PM, often I'd go to *Urban Peak,* an outreach program for homeless youth in Capitol Hill just off Colfax. They were always good for a bologna and American cheese sandwich and a can of soda. Sometimes, if it was raining or I was especially bored, I would go inside and let them "counsel" me for a half hour or so. They genuinely seemed to care and were very nice, unlike the freaks at the "Jesus Slaves" shelter who would make everyone stand in line before listening to an hour long fire and brimstone sermon about how we were all sinners who were going to hell before we could have a bologna and American cheese sandwich. There was also an older heavyset woman named "Mom" who drove the RTD 16th Street Mall Ride bus and would hand out bologna and American cheese sandwiches to anyone who wanted one. I ate a lot of bologna during this time.

Drugs were everywhere on the street. It seemed like almost everyday someone was offering to give me free drugs: acid, meth, coke, heroin, weed. Occasionally I would have a puff or two of weed, but I was terrified of drugs. People were going to the hospital all the time for overdoses and bad reactions. The acid and meth going around was not clean at all. Either someone was making it wrong or it was deliberately poisoned. People we knew as well as strangers were always giving it away, and people were always getting sick, having convulsions, dying. I was scared to do drugs. The zombie couple clinched it. They were a man and woman, junkies of indeterminate age, who looked like skeletal rotting corpses. They seemed very nice, when you could understand what they were mumbling, but they shambled down the Mall like the living dead and it was horrifying. I could never do anything that might result in me looking like a zombie. All I wanted was a bottle of Mickey's Malt Liquor, but when you are underaged alcohol is a lot harder to get than drugs.

One of the first things you need to learn in a new environment are who the players are and what are the rules. The two main groups on the streets of Denver were the skins and the punks, each of which were divided into factions which were further divided into cliques, all of which favored different colors of bootlaces. The skins included a huge contingent of Nazis who were always battling the SHARPs (Skin Heads Against Racial Prejudice) and the Rudies (traditional skins).

Everyone hated the Nazis, but there were a lot of them in Denver and they were deeply networked with a number of far Right extremist groups that pulled bank robberies and assassinated people with submachineguns, so they were serious bad news. The SHARPs were hard Left, Communist in a lot of ways, and took their politics very seriously. They would fight the Nazis whenever they saw them, and everyone carried knives and smileys... a padlock swung from a bandanna or chain. While I appreciated the aesthetic, the music, even the violence, politics was never my thing so I gave the skins plenty of space and gravitated towards the gutter punks.

There were many cliques of gutter punk: crust punks, scumfucks, travelers, transients, trainhoppers, skaters, and poseurs were a few examples. We were the "Muddy's Kids" and presented as more squared away and articulate than the average punk so as not to be banned from our favorite hangout. I was very selective about who I ran with because I didn't trust anyone. Whenever you fell asleep someone could steal your boots, your bag, whatever they had balls enough to grab. I traveled light, with nothing but the clothes on my back and what I could keep in my pockets: a few dollars, a pack of cigarettes, an old straight razor someone gave me.

The main rules were who was cool and who you needed to avoid. While a poseur might suck the cool out of a room, and a deadbeat might try to latch on like a parasite draining everyone of resources, some people and groups had a reputation for robbing and raping people. If you were victimized you could not call the police either, because DPD had a reputation for arresting street kids and never filing any paperwork or taking them to the station... they would take you to a secluded alley with no cameras and beat you half to death with clubs and boots... unless you were a girl, in which case they would rape you first. This was not just rumor... Denver Police were notorious for this during the 80s and 90s, and I knew dozens of people who this had happened to. We learned how the cops operated and had escape routes from every place we frequented in case they showed up looking for us.

I did not run with a solid crew yet, and was alone more often than not. Often I would go to random parties at crash pads just for a chance to sleep indoors. I would always get the couch. The couches were valuable property reserved for the highest status person in the room, which I was not, but I was crazy and would fight anyone, girls or guys, to get that couch. *"But I was here FIRST!"* they would invariably whine... out came the razor, "Fuck

you! Get off my couch or I will cut your fucking head off!"
Nearly every single time they gave me the couch without a fight,
but I needed to sleep with one eye open all night to make sure
they didn't hit me with a lamp and steal my boots. Eventually,
even though I demanded people call me Zan, a lot of folks knew
me from Montebello High as Carol, so I was stuck with the
nickname, "Carol of the Couch" whenever I showed up at a party.
My reputation preceded me and people would warn others to
leave the couch clear for me, which made things easier. *"Don't
you know who that is, fool? That be Carol of the Couch! That
bitch be crazy!"*

19

Sleep deprivation became my drug of choice. I remember endlessly walking, never sleeping, drinking toxic levels of caffeine...

One day, I found myself sitting inside *Muddy's,* swigging from my giant ceramic coffee mug while engaged in a deep philosophical conversation about the nature of space, time, and subatomic particles with several university professors. The conversation went on for hours, becoming more pressured and intense as we argued about the finer points of string theory and wormholes. I felt a hand on my shoulder.

"Sis, are you okay?" I turned and looked at my friends Gimp and Eyeball, bikers who frequented *Muddy's.* I tried to speak and the noises that came out didn't even sound like words. Suddenly I realized that I was sitting on the steps outside the coffee shop, not inside at a table. I had been talking to imaginary people while drinking from an imaginary cup of coffee! "Come on, sis, I'm taking you home."

I rode on the back of his chopped Harley all the way to his dad's house in Montebello and stayed on his couch for about a week until I straightened out. I was unable to sleep for the first two nights, just sat on the couch gibbering while his dad kept asking why he brought home a retard. They fed me, took care of me, got me new clothes, and kept me safe.

Later we figured out that I had been awake for over a month.

20

Over the next few months, I began having memories of what transpired during the month without sleep. More like flashbacks, visions, a series of images without context. There were a few more fugue states while I was on the street, moving through a dream as I stayed awake for sometimes over a week, but never again did I match my record of over a month. Years later, friends would approach me and be like, "Remember that time you..." and I would be shocked, thinking that I had only dreamed it.

One memory troubles me. It is so disjointed, broken, fragmented. I was with two of my gutterpunk friends and a guy we sort of knew stated that he was on his way to a girl's house to buy some pills and asked if we wanted to come along. Sure, why not, it's not like we had anything else to do aside from panhandling or maybe trying to steal a case of beer off the back of a delivery truck. People would invite us to party with them a lot, sometimes total strangers.

This girl had a small apartment around 13th and High Street paid for by SSI because she was too mentally ill to work. She was selling the guy her meds. She was a pretty girl, slender with long black hair and big tits, all the things I wasn't. I immediately hated her. Not because of jealousy over her free apartment and beautiful body, but because something just seemed so *wrong* about her. Crazy vibes radiated from her... I felt nervous, agitated, sick.

I was half asleep and kept nodding off. The next thing I recall was her stripping off her clothes and daring the guys to gangbang her in the shower. She didn't even know the two gutterpunks with me, but they all followed her into the bathroom. It was probably the first shower those guys had in months and I'm sure they didn't wear any protection. The crazy girl didn't seem to care. She was very noisy with her exaggerated moans and yelling, like she was starring in a porn film.

Afterwards, she came back into the livingroom, wet from the shower, laying on her back in front of me, spreading her pussy, rubbing furiously at it, begging me to fuck her. With my short Mohawk, no makeup, and flat chest she thought I was a guy! "What's the matter, little boy? Can't you handle it?"

I don't remember what I said back, but it really pissed her off. Things get unclear after that. I remember her waving a butcher knife at everyone, screaming threats... then I must've blacked out. The next memory I have is the cops showing up, and she has a long bloody cut across her belly. The cops told us they got called there all the time because she was totally batshit insane and they were going to take her back to the psych ward so we should leave.

They let us go without searching us or asking any questions. That one guy had her meds in his pocket, and I'm pretty sure I cut her with my razor. I don't remember any of their names.

21

Soon, I was back on the Mall again. I started hanging out with a crew of gutterpunks and maintained a regular routine.

In the morning we would panhandle. Once McDonald's switched from serving breakfast to lunch, they would toss their last batch of wrapped breakfast sandwiches in the trash and we would gorge ourselves on McMuffins, then we would return to the 16th Street Mall and panhandle some more.

If we were having a slow day, we would look for "Father Faker." He was a creep who dressed up like a priest and collected donations for the Jesus Slaves shelter while yelling about the evils of abortion and faggotry, often in front of *The Triangle*, a gay bar popular with bears. Everyone ignored him except for us. We never stole the money from his little wicker basket, but instead delighted in flinging it into the street and watching the hobos scramble to collect the singles and loose change. A couple of times we even managed to grab him and push him inside *The Triangle!* He would emerge, wild eyed and deathly pale, sprinting down the Mall as if the Devil himself had showed him his pecker. We hated that guy. Years later it came out that he had no affiliation with any of the shelters and was not an ordained minister of any denomination... he also turned out to be very wealthy and lived in a mansion Downtown.

At around 4 PM, we would roll into *Muddy's* and hang out there until they closed, drinking strong coffee and eating nachos. We would often talk about magick and shamanism, the topics of astral projection, demonology, and spirit animals being favorites.

Everyone decided my spirit animal must be a hawk because rather than sitting down I tended to "perch," always crouched and balanced on a ledge or railing while silently watching everything.

We were very spiritual. Some of us were more focused on Native American medicine, others were into *TOPY* style Chaos Magick, I was heavily into Crowley and the *Goetia*. I would read palms, cards, auras, interpret dreams, and occasionally do past life regressions, which I was a natural at and quickly gained a reputation for. People I'd never seen before would approach me at *Muddy's* asking for a reading. Invariably, they left shaken. This was no party trick, I could go deep, giving details about multiple past lives, going back over a thousand years. People started telling me that while I was regressing them my face would change. I kept hearing I would change into a face that was "very pale, like stone, fierce, with jet black eyes." I did not know what to make of that. For years I thought maybe it had something to do with Grey aliens or some shit.

If we heard about a house party, we would travel to that for entertainment, booze, and a place to crash. Otherwise, we would either go to Cheeseman Park to run around all night doing live action role playing and practicing what we thought was martial arts, or we would wander around Capitol Hill. Sometimes we would find a place to crash for a few hours, other times we would hang out at *Tom's Diner* drinking coffee until sunrise before going out to panhandle and starting our routine again.

I was completely reckless with zero fucks given and they would come to me whenever a problem needed to be solved or something needed to be taken care of. This often involved hurting people and breaking things. Soon, I got a reputation for being "crazy." I became the crew's enforcer, alternating between diplomacy and extreme violence, whatever was needed.

One night, we heard about a house party in Thornton but got on the wrong bus and ended up in Westminster, sitting at a bus stop for over an hour before realizing the buses had stopped running for the night. We sat there for a few more hours, talking and chain smoking. Someone pulled out a pint flask of cheap vodka which we passed around until it was empty.

I became paranoid when I noticed them furtively glancing over towards me and whispering to one another. Then one of them said, "We'll be right back," and they all walked a half block away to have some private side meeting while I was left alone on that bench. When they returned, they all stared at me solemnly. "It's time," one of them said, reaching into his pocket and pulling out an old dull Bic razor.

They had decided I had earned my Mohawk! This was a great honor! Back then, you weren't allowed to just give yourself a Mohawk and show up at a punk concert. If you had not earned that shit by being authentic and living on the street eating out of dumpsters, that Mohawk was getting ripped out of your scalp or being cut off with a lockblade. Poseurs who lived with their moms and got an allowance to spend at *Fashion Nation* were not allowed to show up in our scene with a Mohawk or Doc Martens... we would take both, as a lesson to all.

So I got my Mohawk at 3 AM at a Westminster bus stop with a dull Bic razor. Dry shaved, no scissors. The dull blade took gouges out of my scalp and blood trickled down my face. I smiled and laughed the whole time, I was so happy to be accepted, recognized, rewarded... but my scalp was red and raw with razor burn. For weeks I wore a bandanna on my head as a makeshift bandage.

The Crips who sold drugs in Civic Center Park and on the Mall would challenge me, asking if I was a Nazi skin, as would the SHARPs and rudies. I would say, "Naw, I just got razor burn from my Mohawk" and pull off the bandanna. They would wince, shake their head, and walk away.

I was so proud of my new Mohawk. My spirit animal was a hawk. I decided that my new name was HAWK. I was emboldened, energized, transformed. Fuck Zan... Zan was a pussy... no-one fucked with HAWK. I became a walking nightmare.

22

Horse was one of my friends. She was a black girl with long flowing hair like a horse's mane... but the reason people called her Horse was because of her oversized front teeth.

We were in Civic Center Park one evening and Horse came over asking if I wanted to come along with her to a party. This was not too unusual, as we would hear about random parties all the time, often getting rides with strangers miles out of town, sometimes as far as Golden, Boulder, Colorado Springs. Usually we had a lot of fun drinking free booze, listening to loud music, meeting new friends. Attending random parties was one of our favorite pastimes.

Four young white guys had invited Horse to a party, and she came over to ask me if I'd come with her. She knew as long as I was there she would be safe. The guys were all nicely dressed, almost like preps, and very polite. They smiled and laughed to put us at ease, but I could sense they really did not seem to want me to come along. We all piled into a small 4-door car, it might have been a Corolla, and proceeded North up Federal before stopping at a 7-11 up near 80th Street. We went inside, and while they got smokes and beer, I used the restroom. I wasn't inside very long, 5 minute tops, but when I came out they were gone, their car was gone, and Horse was gone with them.

I stood around outside, waiting for them to come back. Surely Horse would say they had forgotten about me and insist they turn around. I waited for an hour, pacing back and forth outside. It was after midnight, there was no bus stop nearby and the buses were about to stop running, I was a hundred blocks away from my friends, I had no-one I could call for a ride and no money for a cab. I began walking.

40 blocks later, I arrived at another 7-11, exhausted and drenched with sweat. With my Mohawk, Sid Vicious T-shirt, a flannel shirt tied around my waist, and a pair of scuffed oversized Docs I'd recently bartered someone for, I was a right mess. I dug a handful of butts out of the ashtray and sat down on the curb, pulling them apart to handroll a few cigarettes with my Zig Zags.

A car pulled up filled with yuppies, 3 guys and 2 girls. They were a little older than the preps in the Corolla and better dressed. They went into the 7-11, laughing and smiling, except for the driver who walked over to me. "Are you alright? Do you need a ride home?" he asked.

"I don't have a home, I'm homeless... but a ride back Downtown would be great."

"Let me go ask my friends if they're okay with that." He went into the store. A few minutes later they said I could come with them. The back seat was crowded, but I was able to squeeze in. Everyone seemed very nice, but it was obvious a few of them were uncomfortable.

After he dropped everyone off at their houses, he started driving North on Wadsworth... the opposite direction from Downtown. "Hey, I'm really tired... you can crash on my couch... I'll drop you off Downtown when I go to work in the morning, is that okay?" What could I say, it wasn't like I had much choice in the matter, and if he tried to rape me I could just slit his throat or something.

He had a really upscale condo in Broomfield and was a perfect gentleman, bringing me a pillow and blanket for the couch, making me a sandwich to eat, and sat up asking questions about what it was like on the streets before he went to his room. After he closed the door, I could hear him opening and shutting drawers for what seemed like an excessive amount of time...

followed by the sound of him loading a magazine into a pistol and racking the slide.

I half expected him to come out and murder me, but he did not. I lay in the dark, staring at the ceiling, listening for noises, until I finally drifted asleep.

In the morning, he drove to another 7-11 and gave me a large coffee, 2 packs of Marlboro, and $20. He dropped me off Downtown as promised without ever making a single inappropriate remark. For years I was affected by this random act of kindness. I wish I could remember his name.

Horse never made it back. No-one knew where she was. A few weeks later, her nude body was found floating in a lake North of Denver. She had been gang raped, strangled, and shot once in the back of the head. No-one ever found out who did it, and I could not provide a good description of the four preps or their car... they just looked like generic preppies in a generic small white car. I think they were probably a different type of Nazi... not skinheads, but Nazis with money. RIP Horse.

23

I went crazy for a while after that. There's a lot I don't
remember... memories of that time are fragmented, like a
scattering of snapshots... I remember sitting down with my crew
and having really intense discussions in which I told them things
we needed to do, but I can't remember what was said. I
remember we had knives and smileys... a padlock swung from a
choke chain collar. I remember looking for people, hiding in the
shadows, and a lot of running.

We would have confrontations with other groups of street kids
sometimes. Often it was due to a misunderstanding, an
accusation, or an old grudge. Sometimes it was due to blatant
disrespect. Occasionally someone would try to rip us off, or
accuse us of doing the same to them. And then there were the
poseurs who usually hung out at the upscale coffee house, *Paris
on the Platte*, with their credit cards and trust funds who just
needed to get the shit kicked out of them on general principal
when they showed up at a punk show... but the worst problems
were with the scumfucks.

Gutterpunks like us were considered beneath crust punks, who
usually were into the music scene and lived indoors, often having
their lifestyle financed via a trust fund... but scumfucks were the
lowest of the low. They were completely antisocial, belligerent,
aggressive, and dirtier than any of us. A lot of them had travelled
here from other states, often by hopping trains. They were the
ones who did the most drugs, drank the most booze, robbed the
most people, and would start fights with random people for no
reason at all except they were bullies. Most of them weren't even

teenagers, but were grown men. The women who ran with them were meaner and crazier and started most of the problems.

Scumfucks often ran solo, because they didn't get along with anyone due to their unstable combination of addiction, mental illness, and poor impulse control... but sometimes they would band together in a group and became far more dangerous. When they decided to hang out on a particular block, we would do our best to avoid them... but sometimes they would walk down the Mall just looking for trouble.

If someone handed a cigarette to a friend and a scumfuck saw it, he would get in their face and yell "WHERE'S MINE?" before snatching the whole pack away and punching them in the face. This was the type of situation we had to deal with. There was no reasoning with a scumfuck piece of shit, no negotiation, you just needed to hit them with your smiley and hope that you didn't get shanked by one of their friends.

A lot of shit went down right in front of the Capitol in Civic Center Park. That place was hopping all night, with gangbangers selling crack, meth, heroin to the hobos. Both the Crips and the Bloods would slang in that park, but never at the same time, almost as if they had agreed it was neutral territory and they'd scheduled certain days.

One night some of the Bloods were acting the fool, talking trash to people, and said some shit to us. Words were exchanged. I forget what I said, but it really pissed them off. Suddenly, one of them whipped out a chrome plated 9mm pistol and pointed it at my head.

I stepped forward. "Promise? Or are you just making idle threats, bitch?" I stepped closer until the muzzle of the gun was pressed against my forehead. "You gonna make my dreams come true? 'Cause I'm ready to go! Pull that trigger!" He looked confused, maybe even a little scared... then he smiled and put the gun back under his shirt.

"Sheeeeeit... bitch, you be crazy." Another Blood declared that I was "alright" and should hang out with them. They lit up a blunt and shared it with us.

A lot of disputes were resolved that way. One night, a guy we knew was upset that the skinheads had sold him bad acid that sent his girlfriend to the hospital. We all decided to go with him to yell at the Nazis. They had a house they squatted at, and instead of there only being 2 or 3 there was about a dozen of them because they were having a party, and they were all drunk. They weren't just run of the mill Nazi skinheads either, but Aryan Nations.

So the five of us walk in there, uninvited, yelling about getting ripped off, and the next thing you know a bunch of guns are being pointed at us. Big guns too. We didn't have any guns and it looked like we were all gonna die, but we weren't backing down. Things were really tense, but the conversation continued and I was surprisingly diplomatic. The Nazis started exchanging looks and nodding... and then they gave us all beers and everything was cool again... they replaced the guy's drugs and even said they were sorry.

Word got around that I gave zero fucks about having guns pointed in my face and was able to talk my way out of bad situations, so my reputation on the street was solid.

24

In the game, *Vampire, The Masquerade*, there was a character class known as "Gangrels." These were unsophisticated savage vagrant vampires that would dive out of the bushes to attack random passers by and drain their blood. That game did not come out until 1991, but back in the late 1980s it seemed as if our gutter punk crew had been based on a similar concept when we started mugging people in Cheeseman Park.

We never attacked women, that was one of our few rules, only guys... usually the well dressed gay guys who would cruise the park for anonymous sex, because they always had cash and drugs in their pockets and were afraid to call the police. We gave zero fucks about getting caught or killed, nor did we give a fuck about our victims waking up with no shoes and a headache. We just didn't care.

I wore a long black trenchcoat and would perch on a tree branch over one of the bike paths waiting for someone to pass underneath, while the other 5 members of the Gangrel Crue would hide in other tactical spots nearby, ready to ambush people who bypassed my tree. When I jumped on them, the long trenchcoat would flap upwards and I pretended it was wings. I had a choke chain dog collar I wore, which I would hold in my hands, wrapping around their neck and twisting it over and over, garroting them until they passed out and "did the chicken," twitching, convulsing, sometimes peeing their pants, and then they lay still.

We would go through their pockets, usually finding ecstasy, coke, meth, acid which we could sell, or bills in their wallet which we would take. We never stole identification or messed with credit cards at all, just the cash and drugs. This was before cellphones, everyone had pagers back then, which were worthless to us. Everyone in Cheeseman was white so we didn't see much gold, but we would take silver chains, rings, watches, leather jackets, cowboy boots to the pawn shop... because back then pawn shops never checked ID. If the pawn shop didn't want something we would try bartering it for a pack of smokes or some beers. We rarely made any real money doing this, as we split everything between a half dozen of us. We would wear disguises... thrift store wigs and heavy makeup... wiping off the makeup afterwards and hiding the wigs behind a bush to collect later.

Because we were "vampires," I would sometimes pull a tiny spike from my necklace and stab them on top of the shoulder, and we'd take turns drinking their blood. We must've done this almost a dozen times, and I am amazed we never contracted HIV or hepatitis C. We had "minions" at *Muddy's* who would cut themselves for us whenever we asked, but it always felt better to hunt, as far as we were concerned. Nonconsensual bloodletting of strangers in the park was crazy reckless, but we didn't think so at the time. We were being "authentic" as far as we were concerned.

Occasionally one would fight and it would take all six of us to take them down. Sometimes they would hold one while I garroted them, or someone would apply a sleeper hold or just knock them the fuck out with a sucker punch to the jaw. A few times they woke up when I poked them, and we would need to knock them out again.

Another thing we would perpetrate was drug rip-offs. We never sought chumps out, they would approach us. "Hey man, can you score some blow?" Of course we could! We knew where several apartment buildings with unlocked lobbies were. We would take their money and tell them we'd be right back, because we couldn't bring them up to our dealer in case they "might be co-operating with the police." Then we would dart out the back door and run down the street. If they were hesitant to hand over the money because we might be scamming them, one of us would wait outside with him. 15 or 20 minutes later they would be like, "This is taking too long, I'm going to go see what's going on." Then they would run out the back door too and we would meet up somewhere, usually at *Muddy's*, and indulge in a large nacho platter, which would easily feed 4 or 5 of us.

It wasn't always violent. Often, we'd just crowd around some drunk walking home and ask for their money and jewelry, and they'd just hand it over without a fight, then we'd run away.

Sometimes we would lurk outside the gay bar *The Metro* (which later became *Club Onyx, Benders Tavern, Quixote's,* then *Black Box*). Only one of us was old enough to get inside, and he would select our victim, someone who was flashing bills and spending a lot on drinks. One night he came outside, eyes wide. "The tall black guy in the white cowboy hat is carrying a wad of hundred dollar bills!" Holy shit, the mother lode! We had never had a haul like that!

We split up. Half of us hung out, pretending we were drunk, laughing and playing around... the others lurked in an alley half a block ahead. When he came out of the bar I was impressed by the wide brimmed Stetson he wore. We carefully began following, being sure to keep our distance, but our excitement over all that money must've been obvious. He turned, stared at us for a moment, then sprinted down Pennsylvania Avenue! I let out the signal whistle and our guys stepped out of the alley and he blew past them, doubling his speed. We ran after that motherfucker for blocks and blocks, around corners and through alleys... he jumped over a short chain link fence like it was nothing, which slowed us down a bit, but relentlessly we pursued. Eventually, he ran into the lobby of an upscale building with cameras and a security guard, so we needed to abort mission. We ran after that motherfucker for over a mile, and not once did he lose his hat.

We heard rumors through the grapevine that the Guardian Angels were looking for a gang that was mugging people in Cheeseman Park, but we laughed. None of them carried weapons, most were out of shape, and their red berets and bright white T-shirts made them easy to spot. We called them "The Tampons" due to the color combination of their distinctive uniforms. We did not care about those bitch motherfuckers.

One night, we were in the park, standing in a circle while I was debriefing everyone on recent ambushes, going over mistakes which had been made and new tactics to try. Suddenly, Blade made a strange gesture with his hand and everyone sunk to one knee and bowed their head in the middle of my speech. Everything went silent.

"What the fuck is this?" I asked.

"We have all decided that from now on you are our leader." Blade said.

"No, this is stupid, we're all equals here... get up." Reluctantly, they complied.

A week later a new kid started coming around *Muddy's* and wanted to hang out with us. He talked a lot of shit about what a badass he was, and one of the Crue knew him from school and confirmed some of it. He also claimed to be a "vampire" and wanted to come to Cheeseman Park with us to hunt. I thought he was a poseur because he listened to *Stryper*, so that was the name I gave him. I had a real bad feeling about letting him join us, but his friend assured us he was cool.

The next night we took him with us. He seemed excited to put on the heavy makeup and thrift store wig disguise and crouch behind a bush to ambush someone, steal their shit, and drink their blood. I think he thought we were playing a game, LARPing or some shit. When our victim approached a signal was given to get ready... and Stryper flipped out, pulled his little pocketknife, and stabbed the guy next to him! It was like he was an autistic having a panic attack, and maybe he was, but he certainly wasn't one of us. We kicked the living shit out of him, breaking ribs with our boots and stomping on his head while our intended victim let out a screech and ran away. We left Stryper on the ground for dead. He was still breathing when we left. I found blood and hair in the cleats of my Docs.

25

We took our friend to the ER at Denver Health with a stab wound in his side. It turned out not to be very deep and didn't hit anything important, although it bled a lot and hurt like hell. The hospital called the police, and he told them a crazy hobo did it somewhere Downtown near the shelters. He was released later that night.

Later, we heard that someone found Stryper in the park and called an ambulance. He spent a few days in the hospital before being sent home. Unlike us, he had a place to live... a studio apartment paid for by a trust fund, apparently, since he didn't work.

I went to visit him because we assumed he was going to snitch, if he hadn't already. I was very surprised he actually buzzed me into the building and agreed to meet with me. I wasn't sure of the best way to handle this... his parents had money, a lot of people knew him, and he had been seen at *Muddy's* with us, so if he was murdered or disappeared the cops would take it seriously and we would be suspects.

I asked him how he was feeling and pretended to care. I lied and claimed I had nothing to do with his beating, and that we were just playing a prank expecting he would chicken out and run away, not intending to actually mug anyone. He seemed to believe me and was worried he would be arrested for stabbing our friend. "Snitches get stitches," I told him. "As long as you don't try to get us in trouble, no-one will ever tell the cops what you did." He seemed relieved and thanked me.

That was the end of our excursions in Cheeseman Park. Stryper knew our secret, our cover was blown, we could never mug people there again. I miss jumping out of trees on motherfuckers.

26

We continued meeting up at *Muddy's*, panhandling, and eating McMuffins out of the dumpster everyday.

Mom passed away due to medical complications and we heard she was having a funeral service, so every street kid she ever gave a bologna and cheese sandwich to on the RTD Mall Ride showed up to pay their respects... at least fifty of us anyway. Her family was from rural Idaho Springs and very shocked to see us. They did not understand why we were there and tried to turn us away. We ignored them and sat down for the service. It was a full house and everyone behaved. Her family was too terrified to speak to any of us. She helped a lot of kids through her generosity and kindness. RTD probably would've fired her if they'd known she was feeding us and letting us ride the bus all day to keep warm during the Winter. She was a saint, as far as we were concerned.

We grew bored, agitated, angry. Instead of jumping out of trees on passersby in Cheeseman, we started lurking around the viaduct and patrolling the Platte, pushing bums in the river and rummaging through their campsites. We never found anything of value, just garbage and dirty clothes. They were like the trolls under the bridge, always yelling crazy shit and threatening us when we walked down "their" bike path. Fuckers deserved to be pushed in the Platte.

We haunted the Silos as well. The Silos were an abandoned building with several old grain silos where hobos, junkies, and runaways would camp. People ODed there and occasionally were raped or murdered. Kids would fall through the rotted floorboards to the concrete below every now and then. We saw a drunk stagger into an elevator shaft and fall to his death once. Nobody really knew who he was, and there was no way to get to him, and we didn't want to get in trouble, so nobody bothered walking to a payphone because fuck that guy.

Sometimes kids would run away for stupid reasons, like their mom told them they weren't allowed to go to a party with their friends or some shit, so they take off for a week to "show them" in hope that they would worry and give them whatever they demanded upon their return. They called being out on the streets "camping." They always stood out because they were smiling and clean with their designer backpack and venti mocha latte, acting silly on the Mall and listening to the alcoholic pedophile bums like they were some sort of wise mystic gurus. Sometimes they would show up at the Silos. The old grain silo was one of the safest and most comfortable of spots to sleep... but you needed to climb down there with a knotted rope. We would see them down there sharing a joint and an artesian organic vegan lunch tray... whereupon we would pull up their rope and steal it. "HEY! WE CAN'T GET OUT! GIVE US BACK OUR ROPE!" they would demand, indignantly. We would laugh, mockingly, and urinate over the side to screams of horror.

Eventually, after several more bodies were removed and the place caught fire again, the Silos were boarded up and a slab of concrete was placed over the main entrance. This made it a lot more difficult to get inside and it was very dark. Most of the street kids were scared to go there now, claiming there were shadow people in the basement who would reach out and touch them. This was absolutely true. I saw them many times, but they never bothered or touched me. They were very distinct, and sometimes I would see colors and faces. They were probably the ghosts of those who had died there. The more scared someone was, the worse the ghosts would torment them. Some people were shoved, grabbed, scratched. But they never messed with me. They always showed me respect.

I have a lot of blanks about my time at the Silos. We spent a lot of time there, and a lot of important pivotal things occurred, but I can't remember. It is blocked. There are memories about this place I just can't access. Not things that were done to me, but things that I did to others. I never killed anyone in the Silos, but I was a very angry person who took joy in cruelty. I was also cruel to myself. We would play games that involved cutting ourselves with knives, burning ourselves with cigarettes. I cannot remember what I did to people there. It was all like a dream to me. Trying to remember is painful.

27

There was a creep who used to frequent *Muddy's* named Adam... but his street name was "Christian." He was a tall lanky scarecrow in his late 20s with wavy black hair he added a lot of product to, with a prominent adam's apple that bulged like he tried to swallow a hamster.

He always wore black, often with a trenchcoat, and liked to pretend he was a vampire. He loved creeping on the teenaged girls, acting all spooky and mysterious as he attempted to seduce them.

It was very important to Christian that people knew he was a vampire... he made a point of announcing this to everyone in his weird lilting voice.

One day, staring intently into my eyes, he stated he wanted me to go with him so he could turn me into a real vampire. "Okay," I said. I don't know why I left with him, maybe I was hypnotized. Gimp saw us leave together and quickly followed.

"Hey sis, what's up?"

"Christian says he can turn me into a vampire."

"That sounds kinds stupid... I've gotta see this shit."

Upon arriving at his apartment, he offered us each a glass of red wine. He had a black cat with big yellow eyes named Gabriel. I liked the cat. Soon, I felt woozy, as if the wine had been drugged... I'd only had a few sips and felt out of it, dazed, as if I might pass out. Christian pulled my shirt off, I was wearing a bra underneath and didn't react. I remember staring at Gimp, opening up my mouth, but no words came out. Christian knelt down, slobbering all over my neck, and Gimp slapped him across the face. I don't remember much after that. Gimp yelling, Christian blubbering, a ride on the back of a Harley to Rob's girlfriend's house in Golden...

A couple weeks later I saw Christian again at *Muddy's*, trying to impress the teenaged girls with his spooky vampire act. He would stoop over, sort of hunchbacked, hiding his face behind his arm like Nosferatu. His affectations were all very dramatic and rather silly. I boldly approached.

"Hey Christian... you say you're a real vampire, right? Let's go on a hunt." He looked confused.

"What do you mean?" I leaned in, sneering.

"I mean, let's go for a walk, hunt down a victim, and drink their blood." His eyes lit up.

"Ah, yes! A lovely night for a walk! I shall be delighted to accompany you on this hunt!" We went for a long walk, behind *Rock Island*, towards the viaduct, him chattering away in a delusional monologue trying to be all spooky like he was LARPing at being a vampire. I intended to do this for real.

Soon, we saw a young couple walking along the path. I pointed at them. "I'll take the guy, you take the girl. Are you ready?"

"What? What do you mean?" he asked... then he saw the choke chain in my hands and went pale.

"Quick! We need to jump them before they get away! You said you wanted to go on a hunt, right? We're gonna drink their blood!" His face crumbled. He stammered. He looked like he was about to shit his pants.

"I... I... I don't think I can do this! I would like to go home now." he sniveled, before turning his back and scampering away without another word. I watched the couple walk out of sight and laughed. I really had no intention of jumping them and draining their blood, but I would not have hesitated to do so to prove my point if he didn't chicken out like I knew he would. I wanted to humiliate him by exposing him as a fraud.

Every time I saw him at *Muddy's* after that and he was pulling his ridiculous vampire shtick, I would walk over while he was trying his best to impress the girls, lean into his face, and yell "FAKE!" before laughing and walking away. Eventually, he stopped coming around.

A year later, while walking near his apartment, I saw his cat in the alley. He needed to be brushed. "Hello Gabriel," I said, and he came over to me. I picked him up and walked away. He was my cat now.

28

There was a hooker on the 16th Street Mall who would hang out with the street kids sometimes. She always dressed in skimpy outfits and wore stripper shoes. I can't remember her name.

One night we started having a conversation about spiritual matters, and she claimed there was a man who had control over her because he had stolen part of her soul. I told her that sounded like bullshit, so she insisted I come home with her to meet him. And that is how I met Attitude.

Attitude was a big angry guy, but he was always quiet. He looked like an evil Silent Bob with a salt and pepper Mohawk that was usually tied back in a ponytail under a black watch cap. He always wore black clothes under an Army green trenchcoat. He was like a shadow, always lurking in the background, nearly invisible, moving through a room without a sound.

They lived together in a small, Capitol Hill, garden level apartment. The air was musty and stale, the one bedroom heaped to the ceiling with trash, and there was no electricity so it was always dark. I do not know if the water still worked or not. The place was filthy, and there were roaches everywhere. The front door was left open a lot.

Attitude looked at me, assessing but not acknowledging. He did not speak to me at all. I talked with his girlfriend for a while and ended up sleeping on the couch. I woke up to him fucking her on the floor next to me.

I would stop by to crash several times a week, because they never said I couldn't and it was better than a park bench. Attitude rarely talked, would sit sharpening his huge kukhri knife daily, and gave off this intense spooky vibe... but I felt safe there. His best friend was Phantom, who looked like a heavyset Kiefer Sutherland with a strawberry blonde Mohawk. He would sometimes crash there too.

One night, Attitude brought home a stack of thick T-bone steaks he had stolen from a supermarket. He handed them out to each of us. We tore open the packages and ate them raw, holding them in our hands, tearing pieces off with our teeth as blood ran down our arms. I must have eaten over a pound and a half of raw steak, and it was the most delicious thing I'd ever tasted.

29

After about a month, Attitude's hooker girlfriend disappeared and Phantom got a much nicer apartment which was half a Victorian house with a beautiful stained glass door. I started dating Phantom, whose name was Ray, but remained a virgin because I could not tolerate anyone touching me and trusted no-one. It was a clean apartment with electricity and hot water. It was the first home I ever had, as far as I was concerned, and Ray and Attitude were my only family.

Shortly after we moved in, Ray announced that Attitude would be staying with us. "But where? This place is so small there isn't any room!"

"He will stay in the closet." It wasn't even a walk-in closet... it was far too tiny for anyone to sleep in, but that was exactly what he did. Every night Attitude would crawl into his sleeping bag and stick his head in the closet and go to sleep. A few times I saw him burning an incense censer and candles there, once burning a small scrap of paper in the flames as if he was casting a spell. He never talked about magick though. He never talked about a lot of things... like where he would go when he would disappear for days at a time. As far as I knew he didn't get drunk or use drugs, and didn't have a job, or a new girlfriend... but he always had money to contribute towards expenses. It was clear he had very strong principles... although he never talked about what they were... but I trusted him.

This was the time my kung fu training began. Attitude had purchased a 3 foot long fiberglass blowgun and every time I walked through the room I would find a dart sticking out of my back, ass cheek, leg. I would be very quiet, cautious, quick crossing that room, trying to avoid being shot by stealth and evasion. Sometime I would succeed in dodging one of his shots and felt proud. Eventually he ran out of blowgun darts and began using darts fabricated from pins, thumbtacks, even lit cigarettes. And then he purchased a set of throwing stars which hurt a lot more.

When he would show up at *Muddy's*, he would sit across from me. After a few minutes I would feel a searing pain and realized he had lightly slashed me across my leg with that huge kukhri he always carried. Whenever he saw an opportunity, realized that my attention had wandered... *snik!* I had a new cut. He would palm a razor, lashing out at legs, arms, hands, far quicker than I could react. I became hypervigilant and twitchy. I was tense like a tuning fork, always on edge... no-one could sneak up on me anymore. I became *quick* with lightning reflexes. He had fewer and fewer opportunities, and now whenever he tried I could dodge. This was an ongoing game for him, the entire year we lived together with Ray. In addition, one of Ray's favorite games was to ignite a stream of WD-40 like a flamethrower to wake me up, then chase me out the door shooting fireballs as I ran down the block, screaming, in my underwear. Even though this happened weekly, no-one ever called the cops. After the first few times I stopped being scared and thought it was funny.

Ray would stand on the corner "flagging" with a cardboard sign and sometimes I would stand out there with him. His sign usually said "NEED WORK" and sometimes people would hire us for odd jobs. One time this guy hired us to clean out his garage and drove us all the way to Broomfield. After hours of work, he told me he had something inside he wanted me to clean. It was his dick. I immediately ran out the door and told Ray, "We need to get the fuck out of here right now." The creep refused to answer his doorbell and pay us for the work we had done. It was miles to the nearest bus stop. Ray stopped flagging for work after that. From then on he just asked for cash. He made at least a hundred bucks every time he stood on the corner... sometimes a hundred and fifty. That was good money back when the minimum wage was about five bucks an hour. It was a lot more than we could've made working. Work was for suckas.

Ray and Attitude would get on the bus to sell plasma twice a week, but I never did that because I hated needles. I started hanging out with my old crew again, mugging drunks walking home from the club, ripping off chumps trying to buy drugs, but occasionally someone Downtown needed something handled: someone needed to be paid a visit, have shit explained to them, and maybe be punched in the face or have their place torn apart and trashed. This never paid as much as it should, but it was fun quick cash and helped to establish our reputation as enforcers.

Me, Ray, and Attitude would also dumpster dive and find stuff to take home, or even barter or pawn. When people moved or were evicted sometimes everything they owned was tossed in the trash: clothes, shoes, furniture, electronics, cookware, mirrors, candlesticks, musical instruments. We brought home framed paintings, cast iron skillets, a really nice stereo, but the coolest thing I ever found was a big leather artist's portfolio filled with pen and ink sketches. I would sit and look through it for hours. There was no name inside and none of the drawings were signed. I still have that today.

Eventually, our apartment started to look upscale with our mismatched walnut furniture and brass framed artwork hung from the walls. We even had a television and VCR. We would invite people over to play rummy and drink beer and they would be impressed by how well we were doing with no jobs.

Eventually, me and Ray started trying to have sex. I remained a virgin a while longer because my hymen was too thick and he had trouble getting through and it would hurt so much I'd make him stop. We didn't use protection because he had an official medical piece of paper from when he tried to sell his jizz to a sperm bank saying he was shooting blanks.

The night we finally made it work, Attitude was engrossed in doing some sort of ritual in his closet, filling the apartment with incense smoke. We were listening to *Queensryche* on the stereo and Ray earnestly declared he loved me. He wasn't shooting blanks that night, I immediately became pregnant.

After experiencing morning sickness a few times and missing my period twice, I shoplifted a pregnancy test and it was positive. I freaked out, crying. I did not want to have a baby and couldn't afford $500 for an abortion. I started punching myself in the stomach and researching abortant herbs in my books. Attitude came home and I asked him what I should do.

"Nothing. My ritual worked. I brought something across." I did not understand why he would have performed a fertility ritual, of all things, without even bothering to consult with me or Ray. As far as I knew, Ray didn't want kids either. It seemed beyond inappropriate, a violation. He never explained why he did it or what he summoned, but I stopped thinking about aborting and decided to keep it.

At least once a week I would go for a walk with Attitude, picking through dumpsters mostly. One night we were walking through an alley Downtown and suddenly Attitude stiffened, alerting at a guy leaning up against a chain link fence. The guy didn't look homeless, he was just a young guy with messy hair, but something seemed off about him.

As we were walking past, suddenly there was a blur of movement and Attitude grabbed the guy by the throat and stabbed him in the heart with that giant knife of his, lifting his feet off the ground. Releasing his grip, the man's lifeless body fell to the ground and we walked away. He didn't even search the guy for money or drugs, just walked away calmly like it was nothing. I followed. I didn't know what else to do.

I was terrified... too frightened to say a word... convinced he would murder me too for what I had witnessed... but he didn't. We walked home in silence.

I have no idea who that guy was or why he killed him, no words were exchanged and it happened so fast I must have missed something. Did the guy attack first? Did he go for a weapon? Was there some sort of beef between them?

All I know is that Attitude was an honorable man. He always carried himself with such a regal, distinguished bearing. I never saw him beat or rob anyone. I trusted him completely and knew he must have had a very good reason for what he did. Perhaps he saw beyond the mask and recognized him for what he was?

The next day, he sat across from the table from me, staring into my eyes... then grabbed his Mohawk in one hand, drew that huge knife with the other, and sliced it off with a single cut. My jaw dropped.

He reached out, handing it to me. When I took it he seized me, squeezing my hand so hard it hurt, and his eyes went completely BLACK. Hundreds of visions flashed through my mind, everything he ever experienced, his childhood, past lives, his demon form... then he stood and walked out the door without a word. I was dazed, dizzy, as if I was dreaming... I must have sat there for hours, trying to process what I had seen, but it was far too much, too fast. I still do not fully understand it.

He never returned, leaving his few meager belongings in the closet. All he took was his trenchcoat and his knife. I have no idea where my *sensei* went. No-one knows.

32

Money became tight without Attitude's weekly contribution, but somehow Ray still had enough to throw pizza and beer parties for his friends. Sometimes we would play Dungeons & Dragons, which is how I met "Kit"... a nice fellow with a misshapen skull, like that kid from *Mask* but not quite as fucked up. He always wore a black leather motorcycle jacket with lots of zippers... even when it was warm.

Kit's best friend was a big guy named "Cat." We thought that was funny, Kit and Cat, like the chocolate bar. He was a big guy, with big muscles, and a military flattop haircut from being a former Marine... he also was a former Guardian Angel and still wore his red beret around Denver. Cat had a huge crush on me but was always very respectful due to my relationship with Ray... however, he made it very clear that if we ever broke up he wanted me to be his gal. He was a good friend, but not really my type... too clean cut and Lawful Good, I suppose.

We started going over to Cat's house to play D&D because he had a bigger table and all the books, modules, miniatures. Ray stopped coming after his character died so he ate a bag of mushrooms and gave himself a hundred splinters from stripping naked and humping the wooden fence in the backyard.

One night, we were playing a campaign which involved a forest adventure. Our characters were about to set up an ambush for some NPCs we expected to be travelling along a path in the woods. We had been gaming for hours and I thought nothing of saying, "I am going to climb a tree and hide in the branches, waiting for them to pass underneath... then I'm gonna drop down and choke them out, just like those motherfuckers in Cheeseman Park!" Cat froze. He didn't move for several minutes.

"What did you just say?" His voice sounded strained. Suddenly, I realized I fucked up.

"What?"

"I'VE BEEN LOOKING FOR YOU!!!" he yelled. Now I was scared. Was he going to beat my ass? Worse... was he going to call the police and tell them what I did?

"What do you mean?"

"YOU MOTHERFUCKER! We were looking for a gang of muggers who would drop out of trees and strangle people in that park! We looked for you for YEARS! How did you evade us?" Now there was absolutely no question in my mind that I had been caught. But I just didn't care at that point.

"Disguises. We would wear wigs and hide them afterwards, then we would all split up and regroup later." He shook his head. He was really pissed.

"So... um... should I leave? Does this mean I can't finish the game?" He blinked, looking surprised, as if he had been slapped. He stammered for a moment.

"YOU ARE SO LUCKY THAT I LIKE YOU!" he yelled. We all laughed and continued playing like normal. It was a good night.

I returned every week until the campaign concluded and he never spoke of the incident in Cheeseman Park again.

33

As my pregnancy progressed and became more obvious, Ray started drinking heavily and I suspected he was doing harder drugs as well. He was less interested in sex and began making excuses for staying out late or not coming home. Soon, the electricity was shut off. As it became obvious we were about to be evicted for nonpayment of rent, we moved to a smaller place a few blocks away. It was less than half the size of our current place, so we didn't even bother taking most of our stuff, just leaving it behind.

The new place was tiny, grimy, dark, and infested with roaches. We spent a day carrying over the bedframe, mattress, dining table, and a few wooden chairs. We stopped inviting people over. We were ashamed of this dingy shithole.

Ray had spent all our money on the first month's rent for this place, so all we had to eat was a loaf of bread, a jar of peanut butter, and half a case of canned cat food from when we briefly owned s stray Manx before he got flattened by a car. I would sit home alone, in the dark, crying, eating my peanut butter and cat food sandwich while Ray would disappear for days at a time doing who knows what. This was the absolute worst time of my life.

A couple days later, Ray somehow got some money together and came home all smiles with a case of Heiniken longnecks. I had lost my taste for beer months ago so he was thinking only of himself. He didn't even bring me a hamburger from McDonalds. As he sat at the table, drinking his expensive beer, I asked how much money was left and he reluctantly dug into his pocket, pulling out a few wadded singles and a scattering of coins.

I flipped the fuck out, berating him for what a selfish piece of shit he was, spending all his money on beer while the mother of his child was eating cat food. I forget what I said, it was as if something else was speaking through me, screaming actually, for over an hour. When I scooped up the remaining cash and stormed out, slamming the door behind me, he was pale, shaking, weeping miserably.

I went to the only place I could... *Muddy's*... and ordered the bagel pizza which was all I could afford, and after I was finished I grabbed a mug left on an empty table and took it to the restroom to rinse out. I stayed there for hours drinking strong coffee.

When I returned, all the beer bottles were empty and the dining room table was covered with blood... not a spattering, or even a puddle, but over a quart covering the entire tabletop and pooling on the floor. I followed a blood trail into the bedroom and turned on the light. The mattress was soaked with blood and Ray was completely white, both arms slit from wrist to elbow. He had committed suicide. I stood there, stunned, unsure what to do... then I heard him groan.

I ran down the hallway, pounding on doors, screaming for help, until someone finally called 911. When the paramedics arrived Ray had no pulse and they said by all rights he should be dead, but he was still breathing weakly so they started an IV and wheeled him out.

After the ambulance drove away, I knew I needed to get out of there. I needed Ray out of my life.

34

I reached out to everyone I knew, looking for a new place, and soon arranged to move in with the sister of a childhood friend. I was a couple years younger than her and we both collected Breyer horses. When we were kids we would play with our horses for hours, naming all of them and making up intricate storylines about flying horses, vampire horses, good and evil horses. But as adults, we really didn't have much in common.

She lived in Thornton, at the Shiloh Apartments, so I immediately lost contact with all my street friends and disappeared completely from the scene. I began working at Taco Bell and living a normal, boring, vanilla life until I was in my 9th month and could no longer work on my feet all day.

I made one of the toughest decisions of my life and telephoned Karen. She was ecstatic to hear she was about to be a grandmother and invited me back without hesitation. It was awkward, but she did her best to make me comfortable. I was allowed to move into my old room and was even given back the keys to the Cavalier!

The Toadies were going to be playing at a local bar for only 3 dollar admission and I was determined to go... but my water broke while I was getting ready and Karen drove me to Fitzsimmons Hospital because it was close and I was still under 18 and covered by Lafayette's VA insurance.

I was in labor for 12 hours. There had been nice weather for weeks as it was nearly May, but a surprise blizzard hit that night and Denver was blanketed with 4 inches of snow. They injected me with pain medication when I arrived, but it soon wore off and they could not give me more. It was a natural childbirth and I felt everything... including the episiotomy when they needed to cut me open.

Everyone likes to talk about "the miracle of childbirth." You know what it was like for me? Giving birth was like the most satisfying dump I ever took after being constipated for months. I was so relieved when it was over.

Jessey was born at 0612... with a dozen long red hairs in a perfect line from front to back... a Mohawk! He was nearly 9 pounds and 21 inches.

35

I took out a student loan and began attending cosmetology school at Sharon *Duran's Academy of Hair Design* for a full year, in hope of pursuing a legitimate career goal. Karen had given me back all my documentation as well as the title to the Cavalier. I owned a car! I decided to name it "Ozzy."

Karen watched Jessey while I attended school, and sometimes after class I would drive back to Eastlawn, but also traveled to Fairmont and Riverside. I loved cemeteries... they were so peaceful.

One day I felt compelled to drive in a different direction, and soon found myself near the sacrifice site, maybe a mile away. There was an illegal target range there, old appliances like washing machines and refrigerators riddled with bulletholes, tires, couches, televisions, all shot up. I walked amongst the debris for a while, looking for something, I knew not what.

Then I saw it... a bone, laying on the ground... I walked closer. Attached to the bone was a skeletal foot. It was about the size of a young girl's leg, someone around 13, the age of the girl tied to the tree. I looked around and saw no trace of any other bones. Perhaps coyotes dug up a shallow grave and carried this leg here? I picked it up, and immediately heard the name "Elizabeth."

The bone was sunbleached, but a few scraps of ligament were still attached to the foot. I carried it back to the car, wrapped it in an old towel, and put it in the trunk. I drove home, telling no-one. She was my secret treasure.

36

I had no place to hide Elizabeth because Karen regularly searched my room, so I just kept her in the trunk next to the spare tire.

School was fun. I learned a lot. The only thing I didn't like was the grumpy old ladies who would come in every week for their discount roller sets, yelling at us if we didn't back comb their hair just right.

On lunch break, sometimes I would do tarot readings for the other students. I never charged for this... you're not supposed to charge for readings... but they would give me tips or do my hair or barter small things in exchange.

I did not go out much during this time. Karen started falling back into her old routine, getting stricter and crazier, even going so far as to take my keys away every Friday night, not returning them until Monday morning, so not only was I unable to drive Ozzy but I was a prisoner inside the house all weekend, unable to unlock the barred doors. Karen hated my few friends and refused to let them visit. I was miserable and alone.

Eventually, I graduated and got my cosmetology license. I started applying for jobs and accepted the first place that made me an offer. Cost Cutters: the Burger King of beauty salons.

I had been talking to Tony, my friend from Thomas Jefferson High, and he was complaining about his mother being horrible as well. He was working as a security guard, and we figured that between our two incomes we could rent our own place. We found a fairly nice apartment near Potomac and 6th that had a 6 month lease. We paid the first month's rent and security deposit and moved in immediately. I had regained my freedom!

37

Jessey had his own room, and Karen agreed to babysit some weekends, and my brother lived nearby and his wife would babysit during the week while I worked. I was very lucky in that regard. Most single mothers who could not find a reliable babysitter ended up getting trapped in the welfare system because they were unable to hold a minimum wage job and afford daycare. I was still able to have a life.

Myself and Tony were best friends, but never were romantically involved. We also had very different schedules and rarely saw each other, as he worked nights and weekends as a security guard Downtown and I worked weekdays at Cost Cutters.

I had nothing in common with my coworkers so my only opportunity to socialize was to hang out at *Muddy's* after work and drink coffee with the street kids. I knew a few of them from before, and they freaked out when they saw me after having disappeared for a year. "HOLY SHIT! Hawk! You're alive! Everyone said you were dead!"

"Really? How did I die?"

"Everyone said you beat up an undercover during a drug rip off and got shot by the cops!"

"Cool..." Apparently, I had become a legend on the streets simply by leaving to have a kid. People are stupid.

On weekends that Karen could watch Jessey, I was free to run wild. I had a group of friends I would bring to the apartment every weekend. When Jessey was gone we would drop acid and trip. We liked to listen to *Danzig, Skinny Puppy,* and *Ministry* a lot at this time, which influenced the vibe. Usually it was a lot of fun and I had a great time, like when I saw the floor covered with mathematical equations in red laser light, which I was convinced would tell me how to build a Star Trek holodeck in my living room if I could only write them down. Another time, we all saw small round grey forms with mouths filled with sharp teeth that frightened us... we called them "carpet monsters."

Other times, someone did something to disrespect my home and I would flip out like Mister Hyde... like that time a girl I did not know locked herself in the bathroom, breaking open my disposable razor so she could slit her wrists with one of the narrow blades inside, which seriously harshed my mellow, as the hippies might say.

I was able to shim the lock with my driver license to open the door and saw this stupid bitch all blubbering while ineffectually scratching her arm with a series of superficial cuts. I grabbed her by the throat, dragged her out to the living room in front of everyone, then slammed her against the wall, lifting her off the ground.

"This stupid bitch thinks she's gonna kill herself in my bathroom!" I yelled, before whipping out the straight razor and pressing it up against her neck, lightly nicking her once or twice. "Okay, let's go! I will help you! Ready? Count of three! One... two..." She started bawling, begging me not to kill her, so I tossed her to the ground in disgust. The guy she came with quickly escorted her away. My buzz was ruined.

One weekend I did such strong acid that I was still tripping hard the next day on what was supposed to have only been a quarter hit... and I had appointments for two perms that morning. My pupils must've been huge and a co-worker asked if I was okay. Sure, fine, I got this...

Ten minutes later, after washing the customer's hair, I'm repeatedly running the strands through my fingers, marveling at the feel of the keratinous scales... "Is everything alright?" she asked. Fine, everything's fine... I completed the two perms in record time and they were both perfect... then I said I wasn't feeling well and took the rest of the day off.

On the weekends I had Jessey, I did not drink, roll, or trip, but my friends still wanted to visit. We would hang out and engage in long discussions about Philosophy and spirituality. One day, we all decided to experiment with meeting up on another realm of existence, whether it was the astral plane, an alternate universe, or simply a very intense and detailed form of hypnotic guided meditation, I am not sure. We did this on over a dozen sessions, each lasting for hours.

Jennifer would always start, speaking the words which induced the trance, then each of us would take turns relaying what we saw. It was always the same place: a grassy field with rolling hills, a dark pink sky, and a tall white tower in the distance. We conducted a number of tests and experiments to determine this was an actual place, not just a figment of our collective imagination, and everything indicated that in some way our consciousness had actually shifted to a different plane. We were always sober when we conducted these sessions. Whatever was happening seemed profound enough to keep us engaged and interested for months, but aside from the fact that we were seemingly able to cross over into another world as a group at will, nothing much of interest really occurred. The other world was rather boring for the most part, and try as we might, we never succeeded in reaching that faraway tower...

38

A few months after Jessey was born, I took him downtown in the stroller, talking to old friends in Civic Center Park and walking up where the RTD station now is. I was tired, so I sat down on a concrete divider. Looking down, I saw a discarded braided leather belt from which the buckle was missing and the braid was frayed, separating, coming apart... absent-mindedly, I picked it up and began fiddling with the loose strands. A shadow fell across me. I looked up. It was my *sensei.*

"It is good to see you." Attitude said. It was a hot Summer day, but he was still wearing that trenchcoat...

"How are you?" I asked. He shrugged.

"Now that you had a kid I like your curves... you looked like a boy before." He bent to look in the stroller at Jessey while I idly fiddled with the unraveled belt. Suddenly, quicker than I could react, he'd snatched the belt from my hand and had it wrapped around my neck, cinched so tight I couldn't work my fingers underneath it. He pulled it even tighter.

My air was completely cut off and black spots crossed my vision as he coldly regarded me with those dead killer eyes as I feebly kicked his shins and tried pushing him away to absolutely no avail. It was like fighting a brick wall as I was being murdered on the corner next to my baby's stroller in full view of traffic and legions of street people, none of whom even seemed to notice.

Just as I was about to lose consciousness, the belt slipped away and blood rushed back to my head as I doubled over, sucking several gulps of air deep into my lungs. I looked up at Attitude. He smiled and held the belt out to me. The moment I took it, he turned and walked out of my life without a word, and I never saw him again...

39

I still enjoyed going for drives out East and would take friends with me at every opportunity. One Friday night, after work, I saw my friend Jason from Montebello High in *Muddy's* and asked if he wanted to go for a drive.

I was driving Ozzy the blue Cavalier along Gun Club Road in South Aurora when we saw a light up in the sky. It was a bright white light that was slowly moving. I thought it might be a helicopter. I stopped the car at a crossroads, turned it off, then got out to smoke a cigarette. I didn't hear an engine or rotors.

"Holy shit! Don't get out of the car! That's how they abduct you!" Jason yelled. He was really scared, of what I don't know, it was just a weird white light in the sky.

"Let me tell you a secret. It doesn't matter if we lock ourselves in the car and try to run. They would be able to get us anyway. It would be easy." I was teasing him because his fear amused me.

"Where did it go?" he cried, from inside the car. He could no longer see it because it was now hovering directly above us. I told him and heard a faint whimper. Then the light started getting closer, spiraling downwards in a falling leaf motion, before hovering motionless again. It went from being the size of a dime to the size of a cantaloupe, hovering, very obviously studying me for well over a minute... then it shot off to the East faster than I've ever seen anything move before or since... faster than you'd think possible. And like that it was gone.

I got back in the car and dropped Jason off at his house before returning home.

40

A week later, I was riding around out East again with a carload of kids from *Muddy's*, listening to heavy metal and looking for UFOs. I drove further East than usual, out by Watkins, out in the middle of nowhere.

We noticed a light that kept following us around. At first, we assumed it was a streetlight, as it was small, white, and at treetop level... but there were no streetlights around there, and wherever we went we kept seeing it, almost like it was discretely keeping pace at a distance, but we never saw it move. Whenever we stopped the car it was stationary, never getting any closer.

We decided to investigate. Determined to find this mystery streetlight, we began driving towards it, but the dirt road turned into a dead end. We went back and took a second dirt road, then a third, but none of them took us any closer. Eventually, we parked at a 3-way crossroads on a gravel road in the middle of nowhere and shut the car off in the pitch blackness, discussing what we should do next. Then we heard footsteps... shuffling footsteps in the gravel at some distance behind the car.

We got out of the car to listen. It was definitely something with two legs, dragging its feet as it slowly approached in the darkness. I had an old flashlight with weak batteries which revealed nothing when we shined the dim beam in its direction. Suddenly, I felt a force pressing against me like an invisible wall, an electromagnetic field enveloping us, pressing the breath out of me, like a black hole that wanted to swallow us... and the shuffling footsteps became more rapid, rushing forward as if it were hungry. I felt ice cold panic.

"We need to leave. Right now!" No-one said a word as we all got back in the car and slammed the doors. Tires spun in the gravel as I peeled out, Ozzy speeding down the unpaved road at over 70 mph. I could *feel* something chasing us in the dark, even at that speed. Soon, we reached pavement, speeding West on Colfax back towards Aurora.

It was Summer and we had no air conditioning, so all four windows were down. "What's that noise?" someone asked. We all heard it. The flapping of giant wings. It would come and go, as if something was flying above us, keeping pace, then would dive down to get closer. *Flap... flap... flap.* Then we heard the *screeeeeeeee* of metal on metal as something scratched across the roof of the car! I pressed the accelerator all the way into the floorboards, pegging the speedometer at 85. *Flap... flap... flap...* still, it kept pace.

THWOOMP!!! A long abandoned billboard panel off to the right side of us shook as something heavy slammed into it and abruptly the pursuit ended. We did not stop, we did not slow down, I continued to redline Ozzy as we flew towards civilization. Finally, we saw the lights of Aurora. Once we passed Chambers I felt safe enough to slow down.

My friends lived up in Arvada, near 70th and Wadsworth. We drove the whole way in silence. After we arrived, I looked at the roof of the car under the streetlights. Three scratches diagonally crossed the roof from front to back. The paint was peeled back and I could see the glint of bare metal underneath. Three sharp talons tried to rip through the roof... if it was a convertible with the top down it probably could've pulled my head right off. We all saw the scratches. Everyone was really scared, myself included.

My friends never returned to *Muddy's* and I had no further contact with them after that. Many years later, while telling someone about this incident, similarities to the "Mothman" case from 1967 were pointed out to me.

41

I met Randy at *Muddy's*. I immediately noticed the girl he was with: slight, pale, strawberry blonde hair and freckles, and very very quiet. Her name was Kylie. They were both on the streets and she clearly did not belong there. I knew something bad was going to happen to her, and soon. Impulsively, I did something I had never done before or since... I offered them a place to stay.

I felt very protective towards Kylie and was positive I had rescued her from some terrible fate, so I was completely justified in not even bothering to inform Tony of his new roommates. He would just need to deal with it. It would only be for a week or so anyways.

Tony was really pissed, but to his credit he hid it well. He didn't even argue about it at all. Soon, I started learning more about them and was convinced I had made the right decision. They both were spoiled rich kids from Cherry Creek who were new to the street... and Kylie was only 15. It turned out she had run away for bullshit reasons, because her parents dared to impose a curfew and objected to her 18 year old dropout boyfriend whose dad was a cop.

Within two weeks I had convinced her that she fucked up and needed to go back home. She called her mom to apologize, who drove right out to pick her up, thanking me profusely. Saving Kylie seemed important, urgent, crucial. I have no idea what happened to her after that, what she chose to do with the life that had been gifted back to her, I was convinced she was going to die if I did not intervene.

After Kylie left, Randy remained. He seemed pretty cool and we became good friends. We would discuss Philosophy and mysticism, and he began joining our guided meditation sessions. Eventually, I discovered he had the ability to channel. He was a natural physical medium.

He did not have any control over it. Sometimes it was extremely subtle, but usually there would be a bit of a shudder, almost a mini convulsion, and he would start speaking in a different voice. The first few times he was pulling through a variety of Earthbound spirits, "disembodied human elementaries," as Zolar would put it. They were often confused about where they were and what was happening, babbling, not making much sense. They never engaged in conversation or seemed very cognizant. They generally would repeat a phrase like a loop tape. One woman's voice kept asking, "Where's Alma?"

When it first happened, I thought he might've taken some acid or had a psychotic break, but I quickly recognized what was going on. This would occur randomly, without warning. Sometimes three times a day, sometimes three days between occurrences. He was unable to filter it and never had any recollection of what transpired. He told me that was why he dropped out of school and had so many problems with his dad, because of these voices he couldn't control, almost like spiritual Tourette's. I felt sorry for him.

I did my best to help him put together a resume and apply for jobs, but no-one wanted to hire him, not even McDonalds. During his job search, I insisted that he do chores, keeping the apartment spotlessly clean, but cooking seemed beyond his capabilities. He probably would've done well as a housekeeper or janitor though.

After a couple of months, a new entity made itself known. This entity did engage in conversation, and when he took over, Randy's brown eyes would turn amber... flecks of yellow opening up in the irises... and his voice would get much deeper. He said that his

name was "Frank" and acted like he was innocent, new, human...
all of which were lies.

"Frank" used to pretend that everything was new to him. He
would try various foods and ask so many questions about them.
He pretended confusion and wonder over things like ice cubes or
hot coffee. I felt so lucky to be able to introduce an entity to all
these new experiences, but eventually began to realize he was
playing a game. "If you were actually human you would already
know this," I said to him once. His eyes narrowed and a wide
mocking *smirk* crossed his face. "All in good time," he replied...

42

Shortly after he arrived, "Frank" began appearing exclusively, shutting out all other spirits. It was a welcome change, making contact with an intelligent entity who could maintain a conversation, but in retrospect it seemed obvious he was being deceitful and condescending almost from the beginning, smirking at me like, "Wow, she has absolutely no idea who I am." I was such a fool.

One night I attempted to do a past life regression with Randy. This was something I was rather good at and had read all my friends and a number of strangers with excellent results. No-one taught me how to do this, I didn't learn how to do it from a New Age paperback, it was something I just fell into naturally, like I somehow always knew how to do this.

Normally, I would light a candle in a dark room, having the subject stare into a mirror while I held their hand and spoke the words which took them back... it was different for everyone... sometimes I would relay what I saw, but usually the subject would tell the story, in great detail, before falling back into an earlier life, then another. We usually only went back a few hundred years, but sometimes thousands. Surprisingly, most of these stories were uneventful and relatively boring. A lot of farmers and fishermen, most of whom died young from accident or disease.

Randy's regression was different from any of these. I lit a large red pillar candle I had used several times before... it was a slow burning candle, 3" in diameter. Then I had him stare into my eyes and held his hands... immediately I went into trance and blacked out... that is supposed to happen to the other person.

I woke up to what sounded like him pissing on the floor... *pssssssssssssssss...* opening my eyes, a blue flame was shooting a foot tall, like a propane jet, and half the pillar had sloughed off the side, forming a sizzling pool of superheated wax. Randy/Frank was staring at me with that condescending smirk and bright yellow eyes that glowed. I blew out the candle and stood, walking away, shaken. When I returned to the room and turned on the light, Randy was back to normal and, as usual, claimed to have remembered nothing.

43

I liked going to Littleton Cemetery, but it was a bit out of the way and hard to get to. It had an unusual history, being an unofficial burial ground filled with unmarked graves before being designated as a graveyard in the 1860s... but we didn't really care about that. We went there because of the portals.

It was a strange place. Tiny white faerie lights would zip past us at night, and time distorted, doing strange things. Very powerful energies there, yet we never felt unsafe... it was a sacred place.

Jason, Jennifer, Randy, and the others had decided to make the trip... then Jason said he wanted me to ask "someone" to show up. He said it didn't matter who, he just wanted to see a spirit to prove to himself this was all real.

"Okay, I will put a special request out, but I can't guarantee anything." I excused myself and shut myself into my room for a few moments to perform a quick informal ritual.

I had been working with Mephistopheles a lot lately, and he had proven himself helpful, fair, neutral... his symbol was still on my altar from the last working. I lit a candle, cut open my arm, dripped blood upon his sigil and very politely asked if he could make a brief appearance if he wasn't too busy, because there was someone who really wanted to meet him. We departed immediately thereafter.

There was a Masonic family plot there arranged in a pentagram we always liked to visit, then wandered around the cemetery, leaving unlit cigarettes and small polished stones on the appropriate markers as an offering to show respect. Jason had gone wandering off by himself... after a while he came running back, breathing hard, eyes wide.

"Carol! You gotta come see this! I think someone showed up! I need you to tell me if you see what I see!" I followed him up over a small hill, where we saw a man nonchalantly leaning up against a tree. He was slender, with pale skin and slicked back hair, dressed all in black and wearing a trenchcoat. Reaching into a pocket, he pulled out a cigarette and I instinctively knew it was one of the ones we had left as an offering. He cupped his other hand around it and it was lit... there was no match or lighter. He locked his dark eyes with mine, then glanced at Jason and nodded cordially. Jason gasped.

"That is Mephistopheles. I asked him to show up and he is saying hello to you." Jason struggled with the name, stuttering, unable to pronounce it.

"Hello, Messed Up Leaves..." Mephistopheles smiled, then slowly faded away, turning translucent, transparent, invisible as he slipped back into the dimension from whence he came.

He wasn't offended. Each of the Fallen is known by many names. "Messed Up Leaves" can be his Indian name. It was all good.

We had arrived around 10 PM... although it seemed like only a half hour had passed, when we returned to the car it was 2:15 AM... four hours had passed very quickly... I have no way of accounting for the missing time aside from portals... momentarily stepping into an alternate reality to commune with a spirit... very different from a standard manifestation, we were pulled between dimensions, like something out of folklore... some straight up Rip Van Winkle shit, yo.

44

Next weekend, Jennifer and my other friends came over to do our regular meditation session in our quest to reach that mysterious ivory tower. Sometime during the session, I excused myself to get something from my bedroom. As I turned around to leave, I saw a shadow with a pair of glowing bright yellow animal eyes on the wall, between the two closet doors... then it rushed me, looking like a bobcat leaping up from the floor, slamming into me, overwhelming, taking over... I screamed.

I did not black out... more like I went somewhere else, another dimension, perhaps. It felt like I was swimming in slime, multi-colored goo which clung to me, weighing me down, sucking me in... and the whole time I was flooded with visions. I saw Devon, the man from my hypnotic regression as a child, and realized Sidney had been working with him all along... then I saw their faces again and again, in a series of past lives and realized Sidney was Sidonai... Asmodai... and Devon's true name was **AZAZEL**.

I was fighting, trapped, when suddenly I felt hands grasping my arms and legs, heard chanting, and realized I was laying on my bed and Jennifer was speaking in tongues, attempting to exorcise the spirit, while my friends all tried to help, contributing their energy and support. Azazel did not fight them very hard. The goal was never to possess me, but to show his True Face and anchor a cord. My body levitated a foot off the bed before suddenly dropping, and like that he was expelled.

I felt incredibly violated in the worst possible way, like my insides were contaminated with this disgusting filth and I wanted nothing more than to slice myself open and scrub my insides clean, but that was impossible so instead I just curled up and sobbed. From that day forth I felt an incredible pressure on my Solar Plexus, like an elephant's foot, a crushing weight, and could sense a thick black tendril attached to my stomach, as thick as a fire hose. Other psychics said they'd never seen anything like it before. It was a permanent bond which could not be severed. I felt like an animal in a trap.

45

A few nights later I was having the strangest dream... Azazel was proclaiming how he had been searching for me for hundreds of years, that I belonged to him, that I was his Queen... and then I woke up to those same words being whispered in my ear... everything was spinning, swirling, confused...

During the night, Randy had snuck into my room, climbed into my bed, and was holding me from behind, whispering into my ear how I was his now and he intended to take what was his. I asked what the hell he was doing when I heard the familiar *clikclikclikclik* of my craft blade racheting open... he pressed the blade against my throat.

"If you defy me, I will walk into the next room and gut thy child out like a pig." I was frozen in shock and horror. Randy had never threatened anyone before... there didn't seem to be a violent bone in the boy's body... but looking into those black pits I realized it wasn't Randy at all. A wide *smirk* crossed his face.

"Six thrusts is all I require to plant my seed within thee... ONE."

Nightmarish images, visions, rapidly flashed through my mind as he counted... images of AZAZEL in his various forms as I had known him in past lives... the Victorian days, the Egyptian days, the days we were like Vikings but something else... on horseback with swords, leading an army...

"SIX!"

And then, without another word, he climbed out of bed, walked into the next room, lay down on the couch and fell fast asleep like nothing had happened.

I ran out, grabbed Jessey from his crib, and hid in my room with the bed and dresser barricading the door.

Hours later, Tony arrived home after his overnight security shift. In tears, I told him what had happened, and he kicked Randy until he woke up. Randy seemed genuinely scared and confused, swearing he had no idea what we were yelling about, that he had absolutely no memory of it.

Maybe he didn't... that was irrelevant... neither of us cared and we both wanted him gone. Tony dragged him to the door and threw him out, telling him to run, telling him if he came back he was dead. It was a long walk back to Denver, because he didn't have bus fare or anything else. He did not return.

46

After the rape, I experienced a mental breakdown and lost my job... I wasn't fired, I just stopped showing up. As a result, we were unable to pay rent that month and were evicted. Tony was pissed and blamed me. We never spoke again.

He moved back with the demented mother he'd sought to escape, and I called my mentally ill ex, Ray, who agreed to let me sleep on his couch. He shared a small apartment with his current girlfriend, with whom he would have loud sex daily.

Soon, I discovered I was pregnant and had another breakdown, drinking a bottle of vodka and repeatedly punching myself in the stomach. I had no intention of bearing this literal demon spawn.

In desperation, I called Karen and told her everything. She listened quietly, then pronounced I was a lying whore slut who couldn't be raped... but agreed to watch Jessey for a few months while I got my shit together.

I met an old friend of mine at *Muddy's* who offered to let me crash at the house he was renting. His name was Zephyrus, and he was a slender 6 foot tall albino with long white hair and blue eyes... he appeared unearthly, and practiced ritual magick.

He did his own thing and I did mine... I practiced ritual every night during the three months I lived there. There was an extremely high level of spiritual activity in that house, but only two incidents stood out.

One night I was on the astral and there was some sort of obstacle course I was expected to complete... but there was a black cat within the course that would kill anyone it touched. I was under the impression that its power would not work on me, but was unwilling to test that theory. The obstacle course involved pits of bubbling acid and deadfall traps covered with spikes and several competitors were killed. I was one of the few who completed it, then I immediately woke up.

The next night, I felt a cat's footsteps on my bed, then it laid down atop the covers next to my legs and purred. I wanted to reach down and pet it, but remembered that supposedly it would kill anyone it touched, so I thought better of it and left it alone. This visitation continued every night for weeks... I never turned on the light or attempted to touch it, but could hear and feel it clearly... it was no dream and occurred while I was awake.

Another time, I was awake in my room when the image of a man appeared before me, within a green mist. He had shoulder length brown hair and was wearing a pair of plastic framed aviator style glasses with his hands held behind him... he did not seem to notice me at all... it was clearly a vision rather than a manifestation.

Earlier that week, I had been wanting to connect with the unknown person whom I knew existed and had been seeking my entire life, but had no idea where in the world he was or anything else about him., so I had been earnestly calling out for him in my rituals... and here he was.

Twenty years later, my husband was showing me a handful of rare photographs taken of him during that time, back when he had long hair and aviator framed glasses... he the guy I saw in my room.

47

My brother told me they were hiring construction workers to build DIA so I joined the union and was hired. I started with two other women, spray painting marks on the ground, then was moved to flagging, before finally being moved to the "prep crew."

Prep crew was one of the hardest jobs at the DIA site with a high turnover rate... most workers assigned to that crew did not last a week before quitting. A truck would lay down a strip of tar which would be covered with felt. Then we would use 22 caliber nail guns to tack down dowel baskets to the felt, after which we would carry a heavy rebar grid, nearly 10 feet square, laying it down atop the baskets and wiring them in place. This was the reinforced foundation upon which the concrete would be poured. Half the time the concrete would crack, and we would be expected to use jackhammers to bust everything up and redo it, so we called DIA "Do It Again." We did this in triple digit temperatures for 12 hour shifts plus overtime, 7 days a week, and drank hot water from a plastic tank which had been sitting in the sun all day. A lot of workers dropped out due to heat exhaustion. But it paid a lot of money. Like $22 bucks an hour in 1993, before overtime.

I tried to save enough money to pay for an abortion, but by the time I had it I was already in the 2nd trimester and no-one would perform the procedure. I resigned myself to working even harder, hoping the problem would take care of itself. However, I was finally able to afford my own apartment in Aurora at Jamaica and 14th Avenue, just off Colfax... and it was all MINE with no need to share with a roommate!

When I was 8 months pregnant it became very obvious, and my bosses got angry and fired me for liability reasons and because I had not told them about my condition. I immediately went down to the union hall and told them I was not ready to quit, so they put me on a bridge crew digging ditches, carrying beams, and laying drainage pipe. I did this for another month before taking time off to have the Devil's baby.

During this time, I made arrangements through an agency for the baby to be adopted. I knew I would not be a good mother. Some people can get past a rape, putting it in the past, even forgiving their assailant... but in those visions I saw very clearly that Azazel had been tormenting me for lifetimes spanning millennia, chasing me from one incarnation to the next, laughing, mocking, *sneering*. Every time I looked at that baby I would see *him*. I knew, in moments of weakness, I would lash out at an innocent child who did nothing to deserve it. That was unacceptable to me. It wasn't right.

I arranged for an "open adoption" from an agency. I was given a stack of **VHS** tapes from potential candidates and could choose the parents I wished the child to have. They would be obligated to send me a letter and photo every month for the first 2 years, then give the child my name and contact information upon their 18th birthday.

I went into labor and everything went blank after that... I do not even remember who drove me to the ER at Rose. There were multiple complications... my water did not break, it was a breach birth, and the umbilical cord was wrapped around the baby's neck. While the nurses were handling all of this my heart rate dropped so low I nearly went into cardiac arrest.

I gave birth to a baby girl a month later than expected, on 9/9/93. This date is significant due to the inverted 666 followed by Azazel's number: 3. It was a very clear message to me.

I refused to look at her. I refused to hold her. I refused to name her. She was immediately taken away and was soon transferred to foster care.

I requested surgical sterilization immediately afterwards, specifically demanding that the tubes be not only tied but cut and cauterized. I never wanted to go through this again.

48

I was offered a job by one of Karen's former friends at an exotic pet store specializing in tropical birds and reptiles, which I absolutely loved, quickly developing a rapport with obstinate cranky animals whom no-one else could work with.

Someone had purchased an iguana which grew so large they couldn't handle it anymore. His name was "Sidney" and he was over 6 feet long from tip to tail and about 70 pounds. His tail was half his length and covered with sharp scales, and when Sidney was annoyed he would hiss and whip that tail back and forth, chasing staff and customers away. Like a cat, he liked sweeping items off tabletops and counters as well. Sometimes he would climb up the wall and hang there all day, then customers would walk up and comment on what a creepily realistic decoration it was, whereupon Sidney would hiss at them and they would scream. He never hissed or swatted at me. The owner would yell, "Mousie, come get your boyfriend!" and I would carefully pick him up and hug him for a while before placing him back in his terrarium. Everyday I sliced up a fresh mango for him which I served alongside a can of cat food.

Another customer brought back a cockatoo named "Colonel" because pets were not allowed at their new apartment. He was a very shy and aloof bird who stayed away from the other cockatoos and avoided being touched. Cockatoos are excellent mimics, but the only thing Colonel could do was whistle the opening stanza of "Dueling Banjos" from *Deliverance*. I resolved to teach him something more cultured, so everyday while cleaning his cage I would whistle Beethoven's 5th Symphony. He would cock his head and listen, but never repeated it.

There was also a large conure which I named "Connor" that bonded with me but viciously bit everyone else. He had such beautiful plumage that whenever one of his colorful feathers fell off I would pick it up, clean it off, say "Thank you," and put it in my pocket. When he began molting, he would occasionally pull out a loose tail feather, clean it off as best he could, then pick it up in his claw and hold it out to me when I opened his cage. He loved me and I wished I could afford him, but $300 plus expenses was well beyond my means. I contented myself by letting him sit on my shoulder all day while I worked.

What I could afford was a rat. I purchased a tan and white rat I named "Julian" who was the best pet I ever owned. Whenever I came home from work, he would be so excited to see me he would dash back and forth in his cage and jump up and down like a puppy, whereupon I would let him out to have the run of my apartment.

He was so smart and had a wonderfully playful personality. He liked to play "Tag" and "Hide & Seek" but he never got the Hide part down right... whenever I got close he would be so happy he would spring up into the air. Once, while playing Tag, he accidentally nipped me hard enough to break the skin, and when he saw I was bleeding he ran away and cowered in the corner, the most miserably sad expression on his face. When I said, "Julian, it's okay," he trotted over, then laid his head on my foot and carefully licked at my wound.

Sometimes he would try to get into the kitchen garbage can and I would hear him scrabbling with his claws as he tried to climb up the side. "JULIAN!" I would yell, and he would immediately stop, hang his head in shame, and slink off... he knew he wasn't supposed to be in the garbage.

When me and Jessey would sit down to dinner, I would lift up Julian and place him on the table, where he would walk over to me and lay down beside my plate, never touching it until I was nearly done and would scrape some vegetables over to the edge and say, "Okay," whereupon he would excitedly pick up a piece of corn in his little hands and nibble upon it.

I loved Julian so much. Unfortunately, rats have short lifespans. When the time came and he passed of natural causes, we placed him in a makeshift casket and had a funeral for him in one of my favorite forest groves.

Eventually, some plastic bitch decided to buy Connor, even after he bit her twice. "I will call him Harley!" she said. What a stupid name. I wanted to take him home with me so badly. His cage was near the front window, and my boss said that she always knew when I pulled into the lot because Connor would go nuts, squawking and flapping around, then would immediately quiet down as soon as I came through the door. Once a bird bonds with you like that, if they are separated they get depressed and pine for you, moping and refusing to eat. That night I went home and cried myself to sleep.

As much as I loved the pet store, it was only part-time and minimum wage so I needed to find something else that paid the bills. On my final day I was very sad, not whistling as I usually did while sweeping the floor that night. The store was so quiet after closing as if all the animals knew something had changed. I would never see my animal friends again. Suddenly, I heard something completely unexpected right behind me... the Colonel was whistling Beethoven's 5th for the first time... perfectly.

49

I heard through my brother that DIA was hiring for a "Ground Transportation Cab Starter" position, so I submitted my resume and put the right people down as references and was immediately hired.

This position existed to protect tourists from dishonest cabbies, who would think nothing of charging double when there was a fixed fifty dollar fare from DIA to Downtown. We would intercept the tourists and guide them to the cabs, advising them how much the fare was. The cabbies were not permitted to exit their vehicles and no more than ten cabs could be parked at the curb at any time. Whenever a cab left, we would get on the radio to have them send another... we would also call Ground Transportation Security if we had any problems, because those fucking *habibis* hate women.

"You cannot tell me what to do! In *my* country we beat women like you!"

"Well, you in *my* country now, motherfucker! Shut the fuck up and get the fuck back in your cab or I'll have your dumb ass banned from DIA property for 30 days!"

I got along with most of the cabbies alright. They all called me "Cussin' Carol"... but, with very few exceptions, they all showed me respect. I only needed to have a couple of loudmouths suspended.

It paid a lot less than construction, but in the mid 90s $12 an hour wasn't bad. I was able to cover rent by myself with no need for a roommate and had money left over. It was a good job.

50

I always did my best to be a good mother to Jessey. I remembered every insult, every undeserved beating, and swore never to treat my son in that way.

For discipline we had a "3 Strike Rule." The first time he did something wrong, I would sit down with him and explain why he should never do that again. When he did it a second time, I would take away one of his favorite toys or ground him from television for an hour. If he did it a third time he would get spanked on his butt. I always wanted to be fair and never struck my son in anger like Karen did.

I would get struck randomly, for no reason at all, as a child. She would tell me things like, "If I had known you would not have been born mixed we never would've adopted you" and would scream that I was a "little witch" who was possessed by the Devil. I was rarely allowed to play outside with the other children once I got old enough to do chores, and she demanded that the entire house always be spotlessly clean. She was obsessive about her fancy lacy chiffon curtains and would take them all down once a week to have me hand wash, iron, and hang them. I would need to scrub the floors and baseboards on my hands and knees daily.

If I was done with all the chores and sitting quietly in my room, as I was forbidden to watch television or listen to the radio, she would yell, "I'LL GIVE YOU SOMETHING TO DO!" and open my dresser drawers to fling my carefully folded clothes all over my room before tearing open my closet and throwing everything on the floor. Then, after spending hours putting everything back as it was, she would demand that I rub her feet.

I never subjected my son to anything like that. I was treated like a slave growing up, a prisoner in my home with no friends. I felt like motherfucking Cinderella with the evil stepmother. I was so fucking happy when Jessey wanted to spend hours watching cartoons and rarely asked him to do any chore other than to clean up after himself and put his dirty clothes in the hamper.

Needless to say, I was very surprised when investigators from Child Protective Services showed up at my door in response to an anonymous report of abuse and neglect. Apparently, someone claimed that I was beating my son and he was malnourished because I was spending all my money on drugs... but I had become allergic to marijuana after my pregnancy, quit dropping acid, and didn't do anything else except have an occasional beer.

I invited them inside and they took Jessey into another room to examine him, then looked in every room of my apartment and saw my refrigerator full of food. When they asked if I ever spanked my child I told them about the 3 Strike Rule and how I had been abused during my childhood and would never treat my son in that way. They looked at each other, thanked me, and left.

These surprise visits continued for years, following me through several apartments in both Aurora and Denver. Eventually I was told that the anonymous complainant was Karen, and since they had never seen any indication of abuse they were going to disregard any and all future reports from her. There were over a half dozen visits in all before they stopped.

Before I realized Karen had been the one filing false reports against me, I thought it was important that she be a part of Jessey's life. He called her "Oma" and she spoiled him rotten, always being sweetness and light towards him, which I generally appreciated.

The problem was when she tried to turn my son against me. I would tell her he was not supposed to eat junk food or sweets, so she would give him Burger King and buy a frosted cake. I would tell him he could not do something and she would immediately overrule me, telling him, "Oh, that's okay." Then she would start criticizing and insulting me in front of him, and when I raised my voice Jessey would yell, "Don't talk to my Oma like that!" and she would lean back with a smug satisfied smirk on her pinched lemon face.

Sometimes, when we were home alone together, and I would tell Jessey not to do something, or yell at him for making a mess or talking back, he would say, "Oma would let me do that! I want to go see my Oma!" Oh, my dear sweet innocent child... if only you knew what a monster she truly was.

51

There were 12 apartments in my building and no elevator. I lived on a corner of the 3rd floor, and stairs wrapped around the outside.

My entire living room was consecrated as ritual space, and my antique coffee table was used as my altar. It was kept clear most of the time, but whenever I needed it I could just cover it with a piece of silk and add candles, censer, artifacts, stones, and my scrying mirror.

After the incident with Randy, I wanted him hunted down... I needed a monster to fight a monster... and I knew just the right one to Call...

I lit the candles, burned the frankincense, shed the blood, and pulled several strands from the clump of Attitude's hair to drop onto the glowing charcoal... sitting on the floor in Lotus pose, I clutched that hair and began chanting... a silent mantra in my mind... calling everyone to me... calling them ALL...

I opened my eyes and saw a man standing in my living room... no, not a man... just a face, head, shoulders, attached to an outline of light gray shadow... I did not recognize the face. Was I seeing double? I saw two images... no, three... something was wrong.

I was not seeing triple... there were ten figures between myself and the door... silently awaiting my command. I turned to look at the clock... holy shit, I had been deep in trance, chanting for over two hours! I had never done a calling ritual that lasted so long. Hesitantly, I stood, slowly walking to the door to peer out the peephole... and I saw them... I saw them ALL... hundreds of shadowy figures, obediently lined up in single file, all the way down the 3rd floor walkway, down the stairs to the landing, around to the 2nd floor, then all the way down the stairs to the ground level and proceeding along the sidewalk.

"Holy shit! I wonder if anyone else can see this?" I thought. Then I heard the metal door at the ground level slam, heavy footfalls vibrating the metal stairs as someone came up... followed by a scream, two large bags of groceries hitting the 2nd floor landing, running feet. The older fat black woman who was my neighbor hustled past my door, shuddering as she walked through several of the shadowy figures... she fumbled for her key and slammed the door behind her. Soon, she reemerged, boldly holding forth a cross, brandishing it menacingly towards my apartment as she yelled, "DEVIL, I REBUKE THEE! GET THEE BEHIND ME!" and a few other things, I forget exactly what.

I still needed to complete the ritual. I had Called all these entities who patiently awaited their instructions. I took my place once again, dropped the parchment into the censer, took a deep breath, blew the smoke in their direction, and closed my eyes...

"I call Attitude to me! All of you gathered here before me... carry my message on the winds! Bring me the one I seek!" Then I opened my eyes. All of the spirits were gone.

The black woman next door was a crazy Jehovah Witness, so she had no powers (why she had a cross, I do not know)... but she used to be my friend. We would talk almost every day. I had been in her apartment several times and she had been in mine. After that day she was very cold to me... would actually glare when she saw me... and she never spoke to me again.

52

Attitude never contacted me. The fact that he did not have my address or phone number was irrelevant... this was *magick*.

That Friday I went to *Muddy's* and several people I knew from the streets said that they were surprised to have seen Attitude walking around Downtown and Civic Center Park that Wednesday. "I think he got a room at the YMCA" one of them said.

Saturday morning I went to the YMCA and was told he was not currently listed as a guest (I knew his legal name), then spent all weekend walking the streets looking for my *sensei*. He had vanished without a trace yet again.

The ritual worked, but we failed to connect. That was the last I ever heard of Attitude. No-one in Denver has seen him in over twenty years.

53

That weekend, I dropped in at Ray's new place on Pennsylvania Avenue since he and Attitude had been best friends until they had some sort of falling out, the details of which I was never privy to. I hadn't spoken to Ray in nearly a year. He seemed happy to see me, but had not heard from Attitude and was surprised to hear he'd been back in town.

"Hey, I've got someone I want you to meet! My neighbor is really cool and weird and he's all like into Satanism and shit too!" I agreed to meet him and we walked downstairs to another apartment unit and knocked on the door.

The door opened and I was hit by a wave of foul putrid energy... like from a hoarder, but the apartment seemed neat and clean. Ray introduced me as "Hawk" and the guy as "Raven" or some stupid generic spooky name, I forget what. He was an older guy, built like a beer keg, with long salt & pepper hair pulled back in a ponytail and a neatly trimmed goatee. His face was swarthy, possibly Native American mixed with something else, and pockmarked from old acne scars. One brown eye was bigger than the other and drifted off to the side when it wasn't focused on me... I felt that I had seen him before somewhere but couldn't place him.

He sat down in a recliner, pulled up a tray table, and began rolling a joint. The air felt stuffy... almost curdled. He began talking to Ray in a hoarse smoker's voice... I recognized the voice... suddenly I realized who this was. This was the cult leader who had that naked girl tied to that tree in the fields out East! Suddenly, his gaze fixed on me and he nodded.

"I know you. You were there that night." My blood ran cold. I thought I was about to vomit.

"Oh, you guys have met before?" Ray asked.

"I need to take off... I have some things I need to do." I said, turning and walking out the door. Ray followed me out.

"You really ought to talk to Raven, you two have so much in common." He said.

"I need to get out of here right now." I said. I wanted nothing to do with that guy and was terrified he wanted to murder me because I knew what he did.

I went right home, fumigated my apartment with sage, and took a long hot shower. I still didn't feel clean.

Ray called a few times after that, practically begging me to come back. It was suddenly very important to him for some reason. The calls only stopped after he was arrested. I heard he had been involved in some identity theft scam involving credit cards belonging to customers at the gas station where he worked. I never heard from him again.

54

There are a lot of urban legends about a network of secret tunnels under DIA. Most of these stories are lies, put out there by the Masons to discredit anyone who talks about the secret tunnels. The more outlandish the story, the more likely it is official disinformation.

The secret tunnels exist, that is a fact. Everyone involved in the construction knew about them. They were built before the rest of the airport. I saw the entryways, which were over ten feet tall. They went in deep and branched off, but they were strictly off limits to anyone without very specific security clearances and I never got to explore them. Supposedly the reason was due to a hazardous infestation of *Aspergillus*, known as "Deadman's Mold," which did indeed affect several areas.

A friend of mine in baggage claims had all access clearance, and out of curiosity once drove a golf cart deep into the tunnels on his lunch break. He followed a tunnel for miles until the very end, where it opened up into a huge airplane hanger... but there was no way for a plane to get in or out of there that he could see, and it was completely empty but employees who had asked about the tunnels were told they were used for storage. When he returned from his break, he was warned that "all access" did not apply to the tunnels and he would be fired if he ever returned.

There were rumors about several levels of tunnels sealed off with pressurized hydraulic doors like airlocks which required a special government access keycard to open. Supposedly, a vast network of tunnels was created by FEMA for "Continuity Of

Government," because if DC was ever nuked or quarantined the entire federal government was relocating to Denver... but that's Top Secret, so don't tell anyone.

Eventually, DIA sealed off the entrances to the tunnels with giant concrete slabs... you can see them from the train because the color does not match. Management told us they "filled them all in with concrete." Sure they did...

There is weird Apocalyptic artwork all over the airport. Most of it with deep occult symbolism, and much of the art is sequestered from public view, often in secure areas. Some of the symbolism is not very obvious unless seen from above, like the mosaic tiles and chunks of colored marble on the floor of the concourses, which could only be seen looking down from the top level. In the main concourse it looked like a landing strip under a map of an alien solar system... later, they placed the security checkpoints over it and it is always filled with people. In another there was a Lunar calendar, and in another it looked like a screenshot of the old Space Invaders arcade game. They all had a mural of some sort that no-one could see unless they were high above it.

Some people claim the airport is shaped like a swastika, but not really. If you look at the main buildings connected by the train tracks from above, it looks like HAGLAZ, the rune of destruction. But if you look at all the roads looping around DIA it looks like a human heart with the major blood vessels attached. Due to these two points, as well as all the Apocalyptic art and the fact that they built a multi-billion dollar airport atop an active fault line, I knew that DIA had been built for the end of everything. I called it "The Heart of Destruction."

55

The following weekend, there was a *Cannibal Corpse* concert at a warehouse a block from *Muddy's*. *Cannibal Corpse* is an extreme Death Metal grindcore band whose transgressive lyrics cover murder, torture, cannibalism, necrophilia, and their music is fast, hard, chaotic. They have over a million fans and their albums are banned in several countries. They are known for putting on a hell of a show, and there was no security or oversight of any kind at this sketchy gutted out warehouse... the entire concert was illegal as fuck... I wasn't into their music at all, but felt a compulsion to experience this madness.

I showed up by myself, stood in line, paid a $3 cover, and made my way inside. It was packed. Over a thousand people showed up for this, and most of them were metalheads, but a lot of punks and Nazis showed up as well. All the violent crazies were here. I did not see a single normie. Then the music started.

I was standing near the outskirts of the pit, talking to a friend, occasionally shoving people back into the pit when they flew out. It was crazy, there were fights everywhere and no-one was breaking them up. Fans were climbing onto the stage and diving into the pit off the speaker stacks. People were swinging upside down from the rafters. It was fucking insane.

The King of the Nazis was in the pit, a 'roided out no-necked monstrosity named Dan Ashley. He was so badass he didn't need a scary nickname. He was infamous in Denver and everyone was terrified of him because he was batshit crazy and could snap bones like breadsticks. We watched this monster casually stroll through the chaos of the pit, knocking fighters aside effortlessly simply by brushing past them, a flick of his massive arm sending people flying. I watched him for a while, laughing... it was fucking hilarious.

I noticed him glaring at me from across the pit... maybe he saw me laughing at him? I quickly turned away and began talking with my friend. A shadow fell over me. I turned to see Dan Ashley inches from my face. He had left a trail of carnage behind him as he bashed through the mob to get to me. Without a word, he immediately headbutted me and I fell to the floor.

I lay there for a moment, dazed, suddenly realizing where I was, and that The King of the Nazis had just headbutted me and was probably about to stomp me to death. For some reason, this struck me as incredibly funny and I started laughing uncontrollably. Then he extended his hand to me, as if to help me up. "Really?" I said. I took his hand. He began LAUGHING then yanked me off the ground with one arm and threw me across the room... directly into the center of the maelstrom.

Immediately, I was set upon. Dozens of guys started piling on top of me, punching and elbowing me, then my adrenaline kicked in and I hulked out, fighting for my life, punching throats, clawing eyes, ripping out clumps of hair, kicking shins with my Docs. Suddenly someone yelled, "HOLY SHIT! IT'S A GIRL!" and everyone backed off. With my baggy clothes and long straight hair they thought I was a dude! They started clapping me on the back, saying I was "cool" and "alright"... then I got yanked off my feet and began being dragged by my arm. While I'd been fighting, all the rings on one hand had gotten tangled in some giant Native American guy's long black hair. He began running around the pit again and apparently was on so many drugs he didn't even realize he was dragging a 140 pound weight behind him! I yanked my arm back and a clump of his hair ripped out and he didn't even notice.

I had a great time the rest of the night, then went back to *Muddy's* for a mug of coffee to restore my energy for the long drive home.

The next morning, I awoke to see my face covered with bruises and it was painful to breathe. I went to work anyway. I was only there an hour before my supervisor took one look at me and ordered me to go to the hospital.

"I'm fine... it's only a few cracked ribs... they can't do anything for cracked ribs except bill me."

"You can barely breathe! I will feel a lot better if you get checked out. Your insurance will cover it. Please just take the day off."

So I went to the hospital where they X-rayed me and confirmed they were only hairline cracks, nothing jagged. "Don't wrap it, take it easy, take some Motrin, and stay out of slam pits," the doctor said. It was a paid sick day and I returned to work the next day.

"What happen to you? Why you not breathe?" the cab drivers asked me. I told them about the pit and their eyes went wide in shock. "You do this for fun?" I took it easy for the rest of the week. I spent my time constructing a whip from elastic bands that I would stretch back to snap the pigeons off the rafters because they were shitting on me. It was a lot nicer than what DIA did. The elastic just startled them, DIA would put out piles of dry rice for them to eat, which would swell up and explode as soon as they drank water. Even I wasn't that mean.

56

I was introduced to Serpent through a mutual friend around this time. He was an intense dude, with eyes like a bird that would lock onto you. He steadfastly avoided making eye contact most of the time, but when he did they felt like ice cold daggers. He was so tense he looked like an injun about to go on a massacre spree. Something incredibly dark was inside him.

Shortly after we met, he asked if I'd ever killed anyone.

"Do you really think I'd answer that honestly if I did?"

"Have you ever grave robbed?"

"No."

"Would you like to?"

"What, kill someone or dig someone up?"

"Take your pick."

Needless to say, soon we became fast friends.

The first time he took me grave robbing was to some old rural graveyard three hours away. It was important that the graves were over a century old, because right around the 1920s they started to cover the caskets with concrete.

He was very meticulous in our preparations. We both braided our long hair and tucked it under a knit cap, wore two pairs of latex surgical gloves under rawhide work gloves, and wrapped T shirts around our shoes before layering them with duct tape. We each brought a ziplock bag for our cigarette butts and wiped down our tools. Then we swore a pact that if anyone caught us, they were going into the hole.

We walked around until someone called out to me. Her name was Emma and she was trapped and wanted to be released. I told her I could help, but I would need to exhume her remains and she would need to promise to help me in the future whenever I called upon her. She quickly agreed. And that is how I became a Necromancer.

It took us hours to dig the hole. We needed to pull out rocks, cut through roots, and go down over six feet deep. Finally, we reached the metal casket and managed to pry it partially open. We wanted the skull, but needed to settle for the feet. We were able to remove both legs and the pelvis, but couldn't reach anything else and the sun was starting to rise. We tossed the remains in a burlap sack and left without bothering to replace the dirt... we had run out of time.

With Emma in my trunk, we drove back to Denver, laughing all the way.

57

Now that we had her, I had no place to put her... so Emma stayed in the trunk for a few weeks. I had removed Elizabeth a month earlier and made a lovely necklace out of her. One night she told me she wanted to go out so I wore her to club. Some drunk cretin looked at her and sneered, "Nice chicken bones." Chicken drumstick bones aren't curved, dipshit.

After club, Heather asked us for a ride home. Serpent started making creepy jokes about murdering people and Heather became nervous. Then she joked, "Well, it's not like you have a body in the trunk, right?" Me and Serpent turned to glance at each other and just smiled. She went completely pale. Many years later, I ran into her again at club and she brought that night up. Apparently it had made quite an impact on her. "Ha ha ha, remember that time when you guys tried to trick me by pretending you had a body in your trunk? That was pretty funny!" I leaned over and whispered in her ear that we weren't pretending. She gasped and went pale again. I have not seen her at club since.

Eventually, Serpent agreed to help me clean up Emma. She was quite the mess, practically mummified, with dried skin tight over chunks of dessicated meat. White strips of ligament were still attached. It all needed to come off,

We spread plastic over my living room floor and went to work with scrub brushes, linoleum knives, and a bucket filled with hot water mixed with Spic & Span. It was hard work, and we spent hours picking off the dried scraps and depositing them in a trash bag while we chowed down on our bowls of Dinty Moore stew...

because we were too broke to afford pizza. I ate a lot of canned stew back then.

After we were done, the bones were covered with soap residue, so I rinsed them off in the shower before putting them in the oven on warm, only about 150 degrees or so. The drying bones filled my apartment with a strong peculiar smell... I had never smelled anything like it before... it wasn't a particularly offensive aroma... just odd. It lingered for weeks, even though I opened all the windows and burned through boxes of *Nag Champa.*

Serpent stated that since he did most of the digging, he wanted the pelvis. I didn't ask why. He took the pelvis and one leg, I kept the other leg. The loose bones were kept wrapped in silk scarves and remained in my altar for many years, once I transitioned from a coffee table to an antique black walnut buffet cabinet Karen had brought over from Germany which held all my ritual supplies.

The remains of Emma, as well as others, added energy to certain rituals and I could call upon their spirits to send messages or seek out information I needed. Necromancy is a very useful skill, although it has its limitations. Keeping a spirit as a Fetch saves multiple steps, and if they are not unduly bound or coerced that bypasses several ethical dilemmas.

58

At work, I would amuse myself in my spare time by making notes and sketches of various oddities in the design of Denver International Airport: tunnel entrances, mold blooms, artwork, mysterious numbers stamped on doors, and just the overall layout.

There were other oddities as well... lights and shadows indicating spiritual activity were common. The toilets and sinks in the restrooms were motion activated, and sometimes when I was alone all the toilets would flush at once, or all the sinks would begin running. The elevators would randomly start and stop by themselves as well.

DIA was built over an Indian burial ground. Throughout the construction phase, multiple ancient bodies were uncovered. Everyone would need to halt construction, and the foreman had a local Native American medicine man on speed dial who he would call, who would drive out in his battered pickup to perform a brief ceremony before the remains could be removed. I have no idea how much he was paid for this service, but I'm guessing it was a lot as he always got there in a hurry with a smile on his face.

During construction, I had seen a huge aerial photo of the DIA worksite framed in the office of the Ground Transportation manager, Christopher, a short fellow with wavy blonde hair and a neatly trimmed moustache who was fond of wearing sunglasses indoors. He wore a work uniform instead of a suit, but with a pinstriped shirt and a tie. I was curious about something, so I asked if he had an aerial photo of the completed airport, as

Google Earth had not been invented yet and I hadn't seen a single aerial photo since the airport was built.

His immediate reaction was hostility and suspicion. "What do you need that for? Are you looking for the tunnels?"

"No, I'm just curious about how the airport looks from above. I helped build this airport and I remember seeing aerial photos back then, but nothing since. What tunnels are you talking about?" He simply stared at me, blinked, then walked away. Shortly afterwards the surveillance began.

At first, I noticed a few Ground Transportation supervisors had begun following me around on my breaks. After a couple of weeks, men in black suits with sunglasses and earpieces began tracking my movements... sometimes I would see one staring down at me from the upper levels, talking into their little radio mics. It was all so bizarre. I even began having dreams about these "Men In Black" stalking me, trying to shoot me with a small chrome hollow pipe they would point at me like a wand. They came after me three at a time, with greasy slicked back hair, reeking of menace and Grey alien type vibes. I kept seeing patterns of triangle, circle, square in my dream, and the meaning of their patterns was elucidated, like a secret code, but forgotten upon awakening... however, I suddenly began noticing these symbols engraved in random areas all over the airport... and they made perfect sense.

About this time, I began noticing a number of odd clicking noises and echos over my apartment's landline phone (this was still in the pre-cellphone pager days). Serpent had briefly lived with me and had recently moved to his new apartment, and was paranoid about the feds investigating him for a series of murders he never admitted to and said they couldn't prove. He was kinda weird and I didn't know if he was joking or not, but I thought it was funny he was worried about my phone being tapped because it was probably just normal interference. Anyway, we decided to play a game to test it.

Serpent collected all the human remains which were potential evidence of multiple misdemeanors, hiding them at an undisclosed location, then called me from a payphone whereupon we engaged in a highly incriminating conversation regarding a number of disinterred human bones I allegedly was storing in my bedroom closet, talking about how we needed to "clean them soon." But, of course, we had already done this and the bones were no longer there.

The next week at work, Christopher approached me, complementing my new purple suede Doc Marten ankle boots and asking if they were "company regulated" since we were mandated to wear black footwear. I fibbed and told him, yes, they were. He then began staring at a little pewter skull I wore on a cord around my neck. "Nice necklace... what other bones you got in your closet?" he asked, basically telling me flat out my phone was tapped. Then he smirked. I laughed without saying another word and walked away.

I stopped going for aimless walks around the airport to doodle in my sketch pad after that. I was a lot more careful on the phone too. Eventually, the surveillance tapered off. Later, I heard stories about how seriously the feds took the secrecy of those tunnels. There were a few high ranking DIA employees working in the administrative offices who were out of the loop because they never got the fancy decoder ring and learned the 27th degree handshake, and they found the tunnels and Apocalyptic artwork so fascinating that they were taking photographs. One proudly announced they had gotten a book deal, and another started submitting "tell all" articles to the *Denver Post* and *Westword*. Then they suddenly vanished. Gone, replaced without warning or explanation.

Soon afterwards, the *Denver Post* began printing articles mocking the various wacky conspiracy theories about DIA, claiming people thought the tunnels led to a huge underground alien city and that there was a network of train tunnels going for thousands of miles across the country... but no-one had ever said anything like that, they just made it up to ridicule anyone who "believed in secret tunnels."

Serpent and I went on another graverobbing mission to a graveyard over an hour South of Denver where we nearly were caught by the police. We wasted hours digging on the wrong side of the tombstone and, fortunately, concealed our tools in the bushes before returning to my car. A police car came around the corner and lit us up nearly immediately afterwards. We noticed things had been moved around in the car, as if they had already searched it.

They wanted to know why we had shirts duct taped around our sneakers and were wearing surgical gloves under our work gloves. It was Winter so we told them we had been sleeping in our car and trying to stay warm. The blankets stuffed around the floorboard vents seemed to back that up. They split us up to compare our stories.

Somehow, even though we didn't plan it, our stories were identical. We were there to visit a friend of mine who had recently had a bad breakup, but they had not gotten home yet so we were just killing time for a few hours. That seemed to satisfy them, so they let us go... but we noticed them following us without headlights until we arrived at a girl's house we knew... and when she didn't answer the door, they continued to shadow us until we got back on the highway towards Denver.

Shortly after that, Serpent began getting commissions for his artwork from several famous bands I cannot name here, but you have heard of them... so he left Colorado... but not before returning Elizabeth, Emma, and a few others.

59

Jessey was a little over 5 years old when he began telling me about the Nutcracker. "The Nutcracker was in my room again last night, Mom," he would say.

At first I thought he was just babbling about having a bad dream, but it kept happening, pretty much the entire time we lived at this apartment. "What is the Nutcracker?" I asked. He told me it was a man with an oversized head, big black eyes, a slit mouth, and long skinny arms... just like the Nutcracker doll on Karen's mantelpiece.

As far as I could tell, the Nutcracker never said or did anything other than appear at the foot of his bed and stare at him while he was trying to sleep... at least that was the only thing he ever remembered... but then I saw the marks.

Several times I noticed a perfect triangle of red pinpricks... it only covered about a half inch, and would fade away within a week, but then the same exact pattern would reappear a few months later, only in a different place.

It took nearly a year before I made the connection to Karen's doll, which was the closest approximation a 5 year old boy could use to describe what he was seeing. About a decade later I realized what he was describing was similar to what alien contactees had disclosed under hypnosis: skinny big-headed Greys with huge black eyes appearing in their bedrooms to conduct mysterious experiments, often leaving small unobtrusive marks.

As soon as we moved out, the Nutcracker visitations stopped. 20 years later he has no recollection of this.

60

One night at *Muddy's*, I saw Randy come in. I immediately fled upstairs and had a panic attack. Eventually, I got the attention of Gimp and Eyeball and told them he was here. They knew what he had done.

"We'll keep an eye on him, Sis," Gimp said, reassuring me that I was safe. That's it? I want this fucker curbstomped! They returned to their table with the other bikers. I remained upstairs until he finally left, shaking and crying as I drove home.

I began spotting him at *Muddy's* regularly, but kept my distance as I formulated a plan. A member of the old Gangrel Crue showed up and I talked to him. "I know some guys, let me make a call," he said, then he walked out the door to find a payphone. A half hour later he came back inside. "It's on."

We talked over what I was expected to do. I insisted that I wanted in. I wanted to be there for everything. I wanted to see him suffer, rejoice in his pain and fear. "We can do that," he said.

I uncloaked and let Randy see me, feigning surprise, telling him it was good to see him. He still claimed to have no memory of the rape and asserted I probably dreamed it. I let him buy me a Shameless Pizza and coffee. Later, I let him walk me to my car.

It was quick and professional. Three Nazi Skins jumped out of a generic white panel van parked next to me and beat the shit out of him before throwing him in the back. I didn't know any of these guys. My friend stepped out of the shadows and said, "I'm riding with you."

and rolled him in a ditch," the one guy said. We drank another beer and I thanked them. They didn't ask for any payment, which surprised me. One of them said it was "fun."

We left shortly afterwards and I dropped my friend off near *Muddy's*. I never saw those Nazis again... at least I don't think so... they all kinda look alike to me. Randy never returned. Nobody ever heard from him again. I think the Nazis probably killed him after all. I don't particularly care, I'm just glad he's gone.

61

A guy I knew from *Muddy's* had become fascinated with chainmail art and began making necklaces and earrings to give away to friends. One day he showed us a tiny chainmail cat o' nine tails that was one of the coolest things I'd ever seen. A few weeks later, for Yule, he gave me a full sized version.

The chains were each over 2 feet long, with smaller chains attached to the ends to make forks. This was no **BDSM** flogger, it was a stone cold weapon of war. It was also perfectly legal, too exotically obscure to be prohibited by law. I began carrying it everywhere.

Usually, I would clip it to my belt, but sometimes I'd hang it around my neck, wrap it around my waist, or lay it alongside my seat in the car. I practiced my strikes on trees... it would rip huge chunks of bark off with every hit. I actually took it to a few fetish parties and people would see it and beg me to use it on them. I never hit anyone with it hard... it would split them open and leave scars if I did... but I'd run it over their back or lightly snap my wrist... everyone loved it, saying they'd never felt anything like it before.

I only used it as a weapon twice. The first time was on a Saturday night after the goth club closed... *Milk* didn't exist back then, maybe it was *Onyx*. Regardless, we were dressed goth with the hair and makeup, and this carload of Chads in the next lane were hootin and hollerin at us, alternating between yelling "FREAKS!" and asking us to fuck them... you know, the usual. I had a flashback to the carload of Chads that killed Horse and began screaming at them to fuck off. They laughed and began throwing fast food drink cups at us. *"Hold the wheel! You're driving!"* I told my friend, before climbing half out the window to smash their windshield with the chainwhip. They tried chasing after us, but were too drunk and spun out trying to follow us around a corner.

The other time, I felt compelled to take a nighttime stroll along the Platte bike trail, towards the Silos. The lights were far and few between, it was a long dark walk... I had a lot of shattered memories about the Silos I was struggling to piece together, and it was a nice quiet opportunity to collect my thoughts. Suddenly, there was a rustling in the bushes and a man stepped out onto the path and began closing the distance. Was he attacking? I didn't know and didn't care. The Platte was a dangerous place, people got beaten, raped, stabbed all the time there, so the chainwhip was already in my hand. I smacked that fucker across the face as hard as I could. He was so close the chains wrapped around his head... then I ripped it free. His face exploded... it was too dark to see the damage, but black blood sprayed everywhere. He didn't scream or yell, he just made some bestial grunting noises before bolting, faster than that Black guy in the cowboy hat we tried mugging back in the day. People run fast when they think they are about to die. He went in the direction I was heading, so I decided to cut my walk short and go home.

That chainwhip was the coolest thing anyone ever gave me. I wish I could remember that guy's name. He was an older fellow with a goatee and wavy brown hair who would sit at *Muddy's* all day working on his chainmail projects. I stopped carrying it because it was so heavy and kept getting in my way... but I still have it today. It remains one of my most prized possessions.

62

One of my friends around this time was a fellow named Tad. He was former military and had a good job doing some sort of tech shit. When his father passed away he got a hefty inheritance and a really cool sports car... a customized RX7 Twin Turbo which would do nearly 200 mph. He actually trusted me to drive it a few times, because I think he had a bit of a crush on me.

He also inherited a lot of guns, including a few that may not have been entirely legal, like the select fire G3 battle rifle which recoiled so hard it practically would spin me around, unlike the AR15 which had no recoil at all. But my favorite gun of all was the SIG P225, a compact single-stack 9mm pistol which fit my hand perfectly. He would always let me carry it whenever we went camping. Because he trusted and respected me, aside from him I was the only one allowed to carry a loaded firearm when we were all tripping on acid. We liked to shoot at gophers with tracer rounds that made a bright red streak all the way to their target. Once, during a fire ban, we accidentally started a brush fire and needed to run downrange to stomp out the flames.

I really liked Tad, but he was considerably shorter than me and sometimes was a bit pushy with his unsolicited advice like, "You shouldn't shave your eyebrows" and "You really need to tone it down a bit, you're too wild." He had a ton of money and if I was a user or golddigger I could've probably hooked up with him and lived quite comfortably... but that did not feel right to me, and although I liked him we frequently disagreed on what seemed like small petty details, but neither of us was willing to back down, so there was often this underlying tension.

The first time I seriously tried killing myself I was with him. It had been a good day, I was having fun, we went to the range and I was shooting my favorite gun. Suddenly, for reasons I did not clearly comprehend, I was seized by an overwhelming compulsion to twist the SIG around in my hand so it was pointing at my face and slowly began pressing the trigger with my thumb.

I had not been depressed or upset... if anything, I was happy... but something took over my body like a puppet and it seemed as if I had no control over my actions. I was not in any sort of emotional state... in fact, I felt absolutely nothing and was acting on autopilot like a robot. Tad was in the next partition and, for whatever reason, took a step back and noticed I was about to shoot myself in the face. He calmly said my name, then walked forward and gently took the pistol from my hands and like that I snapped out of it. I was confused and speechless. He packed up the guns and, to his credit, did not badger me about it on the ride home. He did not ask if I wanted to drive.

After that, we never went shooting or camping again, although we remained friends and occasionally continued to hang out. Eventually, we drifted apart. I tried looking him up to catch up on old times, but cannot find a trace of him anywhere. Perhaps it is for the best.

63

It was a multi-step process, as well as a huge pay cut, but I finally was able to get away from the *habibis* and Men In Black at DIA to land my dream job... working at a mortuary.

I had started at the bottom, selling cemetery plots and burial insurance, before moving to body removal, which involved driving the hearse to hospitals, nursing homes, and private residences to transport the departed loved one. Private residences were the worst. Sometimes family members would flip out and try to assault us, or lock themselves in the room with the deceased wailing and crying in an attempt to prevent us from taking them away. Eventually, we made it a rule to refuse to pick up from a private residence without local law enforcement on scene.

There were a few nursing homes I visited regularly, and all the staff and residents began recognizing me with my black suit and blue velvet blanket. Sometimes someone would joke, "Are you here for me?" and I would reply, "Not today."

There was one old lady in the advanced stages of Alzheimer's dementia who would invariably attempt to escape whenever I arrived, banging repeatedly on the metal panic bar of the exit door, which was magnetically locked to prevent just such a thing. "WHEN'S IT MY TURN?" she would yowl with crazed eyes. "Not long..." I would reassure her.

I loved being on call and driving the hearse in the middle of the night to pick up dead bodies legally. My forearms got huge to the point I felt like Popeye. I took great pride in my work and was respectful and professional at all times. I worked removal jobs for about six months before being offered my dream career as a mortician's assistant.

64

I started out learning how to embalm. They taught us dozens of secret techniques we were never permitted to reveal since it was such a taboo subject. In fact, we were even forbidden to tell anyone what we did for a living lest they ask too many questions. But now, thanks to the internet and a series of tell all documentaries, there really aren't any secrets anymore. Everyone knows about the spiked eye caps and screw in butt plugs now.

We would receive bodies in various states of disarray. Floaters were the worst. We were not even supposed to open the bodybag when we got a floater, they were just put in the cooler until they could be transported to the crematorium. One day, curiosity got the better of me and I just *needed* to see! *Zzzzzzzzzzzzzzp...* SPLASH! The dearly departed poured out like a slurry that reeked like a dumpster behind a meatpacking plant. I spent an hour mopping that mess up with bleach and the stench in that room would still gag a maggot. It was horrible.

Another odd thing we would see was when someone donated their body to science... especially bone donors. They would sign a contract accepting a check in exchange for agreeing to Will their skeleton to a medical school. Once you remove a man's skeleton, they become nothing but a disgusting decaying watery bag of shit. They compensate by replacing the skeleton with a PVC framework... it doesn't help. The body is freakishly flaccid and felt like nothing human, and was so gross it would make me nauseous. Fortunately, bone donors were far and few between.

One of the strangest cases I saw was that of a young couple who unexpectedly died while on their honeymoon in Honduras. As Americans, they were supposed to be turned over to the American Embassy to be shipped to America for the autopsy... but the Honduran authorities decided to do the autopsy themselves and declared that two young people in perfect health simultaneously died "of natural causes." They were shipped in wooden crates filled with straw, butchered like animals. Their torsos had been hacked open, all the internal organs removed, and the bodies were filled with sawdust... they weren't even sewn up. They weren't properly embalmed either, so they were decomposing and the limbs were contorted from rigor mortis. We were unable to do any restorative work at all, they were too far beyond our ability to fix. It was obvious they had both been murdered, probably to harvest their organs, and the Honduran authorities conspired to cover it up.

Embalming is simply prep work for the desairologist. Desairology goes way beyond makeup and hairstyling into full facial reconstruction... using silicone injections and sculpting wax to rebuild damaged or missing bone and flesh. Once I began training in desairology I realized I had finally found my true calling.

65

I was a natural at facial reconstruction and could rebuild part of a head to match their photograph. I would lightly tap the surface of the soft wax with the bristles of a fan brush to give the illusion of pores and match the skintone exactly with special paints formulated to match flesh better than cosmetics. Then I would cut a section of a wig to replace missing scalp and trim and style the hair to match.

Within a year I had filled two binders with complements and letters of recommendation from funeral homes across the state. I was given a beeper to be on call in the event of emergencies, and other funeral homes would transport a body hundreds of miles so I could work on it.

One of my toughest restorations was a young man who had died while climbing in the Rockies. He fell 500 feet while rappelling and impaled his face on a pine tree. There was a hole through his head you could literally put your fist through. Against all advice, his wealthy family had insisted on an open casket funeral. I got the page on my day off... it was my birthday.

I spent sixteen hours reconstructing that young man's face from wax, painting it so he appeared almost lifelike. I considered it to be my finest work. Then I called my boss to let him know it was done before driving home to go to sleep.

On Monday my boss got an angry phone call from Mister Wolf, the owner of the prestigious funeral parlor in Pueblo that transported the body to us. "WHO DID THIS BODY?" he yelled.

"Queen did it! It was all her doing!" my boss volunteered, throwing me under the bus, hoping to avoid blame. There was a long pause on the other end of the line.

"This is the best restoration I've seen from Colorado in years," he said. That was one of my proudest moments.

Mister Wolf probably charged that family $10,000 for my restoration work on their son. I think maybe I made $200 from that job, being paid hourly just above minimum wage. It was never about the money for me.

66

A lot of people want to ask about the ghost stories... if I ever saw anything "spooky" working in a funeral home. As a clairvoyant I am far more sensitive to such things than most. Occasionally, spirits would make themselves known. Usually they were just confused about being dead, but sometimes they had a story to tell.

Surprisingly, of all things, makeup was usually the biggest issue for them. Conservative women would complain that the makeup made them look "like a slut," and men would be upset and confused about why they even needed any makeup at all. "Because you look DEAD and your family doesn't want to see you like that!" I would tell them. And then there was the red lipstick lady...

One evening, I was preparing an elderly grandmother for her open casket funeral and was about to apply a natural toned lipstick when I felt a light tapping on my shoulder. A faint voice whispered, "I want red lipstick." Red seemed inappropriate for the occasion so I ignored the request. The tapping got harder.

"I want RED lipstick." I would certainly get complaints from both my boss and the family if I put red lipstick on grandma. I told her no. The tapping got even harder.

"I WANT RED LIPSTICK!!!" the voice shouted in my ear. This really pissed me off.

"NO! You are not going to look like a whore at your own funeral!" I shouted back. "Ahem..." I turned to see my supervisor standing behind me with crossed arms. Suddenly, a tube of lipstick popped out of the makeup case and rolled across the table towards me. I stared at it.

"Open it," my supervisor said, as if this sort of thing was a normal occurrence. I opened it. It was the most garish bright red "fuck me" shade of lipstick in the case.

Grandma got her final wish.

That was a funny story... not all of them were like that. The spirits do not always speak, sometimes they put images in your head to communicate, like a series of snapshots, only accompanied by waves of emotion: anger, fear, despair.

One of the worst cases was a 12 year old boy who committed suicide by hanging himself from a pipe in his family's basement with his belt. I did not prepare his body, that was handled by a girl on the day shift, and she bungled the job horribly. She wasn't very good at applying makeup anyway, and even though she had been told not to on several occasions, she insisted on making all the children look like cute little cherubs with rosy cheeks. The family saw it and was absolutely livid. Not only did their child look like a kewpie doll, but the ligature marks were still clearly visible. I got an emergency call to drive out to the funeral home in the middle of the wake to redo the makeup ASAP.

When I arrived, I was shown into the viewing area, and found the child resting in a $200 cardboard cremation coffin... but he was not being cremated. It was not a poor family on welfare either... dozens of family members showed up and they were all well dressed, like yuppies. They could easily have pooled their money to provide him a proper casket and tombstone, but chose not to. I proceeded to clean off the inept makeup and reapply a more natural look.

Throughout the task, I was bombarded with a continuous assault of images of his short life of abuse and neglect while waves of grief washed over me. I began crying, holding the dead boy's hand, telling him how sorry I was that his mother had treated him that way.

"Did you speak to the family?" a voice demanded. I turned around to see that the funeral director had been watching me the whole while. When I told him I had not, that the boy's spirit had spoken to me in a vision, his face changed and he became genuinely curious, wanting to know more about what I saw. Then, he solemnly stated me that the boy had left a note that simply read, "Thanks for being so mean, Mom."

That boy was buried in Westminster Cemetery in an unmarked grave... simply a numbered plaque provided by the cemetery in lieu of a marble tombstone. It was a long drive, about 15 miles out of my way, but I made a point to visit his grave once a month to leave flowers and tell him he was remembered and loved. I visited his grave for years.

I was his only visitor.

67

My supervisor on the graveyard shift was a man named Bill. He used to be a crazy biker, but married a Mennonite woman and adopted her ways of dress and conduct. He reminded me of the Tall Man character from the *Phantasm* movies, but with a sense of humor.

He enjoyed playing practical jokes on myself and other employees. Once, he brought a battery operated cat toy to work and hid it in a drawer... it was like a raccoon tail that would bounce off walls and spin in circles... it scared the shit out of the guy who opened it. If he caught you taking a nap he would drop a big metal bucket on the tile floor to wake you up. He also liked taking off his shoes to sneak up on people in his stocking feet to yell "BOO!"

He was perplexed because he could never sneak up on me, even when I had earbuds in and was listening to music. He would creep up behind me and I would take out one of my earbuds and ask, "Can I help you, Bill?" I could track Bill's energy... he radiated energy like a chunk of enriched uranium... and we had a solid connection. From the moment we met, I felt as if I somehow knew him before, and he quickly became my mentor and best friend. Much later, I realized he was secretly in love with me. That connection was very strong. One day I told him that I could sense wherever he was in the building, and he decided to put that claim to the test. He took off his shoes and very carefully crept from room to room without a footfall or a creak. I shouted out every time he changed rooms and where in that room he was.

One weekend, I took a nap in the early evening and woke up in Bill's house. I had never visited Bill's house before, but knew that was where I was. He was sitting in the dining room, which was faintly illuminated by a dimly lit lamp. His children walked past me to go to their rooms, his wife was in the kitchen which was only lit by the oven light, and his German Shepherd on the porch barked incessantly at me from behind the window. Bill was eating a piece of fried chicken and drinking something cold from a red plastic cup... I could see the condensation on the side. He looked up, surprised to see me, then smiled. "Would you like to join me?" he asked. I shook my head, then suddenly woke up back in my bed.

When I returned to work on Monday, I was uncertain how to broach the subject as Bill had made no mention of it, so finally I asked, "How was your chicken the other night?"

"Good... hey, how did you know we had chicken?" I told him what I'd seen and he seemed to have no memory of it, but asked me questions about what his house looked like, to describe his family, and what he was drinking.

"I don't know... it was something cold in a red plastic cup." Then I proceeded to describe his house, his wife, his kids, and his dog. He nodded his head for a while.

"I was drinking lemonade out of that cup. We rarely have fried chicken, but it was late and my wife didn't feel like cooking so I brought home a bucket of KFC. May I ask you a favor?"

"What's that?"

"Could you knock next time?"

68

A few days later, Bill asked if I would like to visit and have dinner with his family. I had been working at the funeral home for 2 years and this was the first time he'd asked me to meet him outside of work. At least once a week he would bring in a homemade pie baked by his wife that he would share with me, and they were the best pies I'd ever had in my life. Of course I agreed.

Because I was in my 20s and kind of an obnoxious asshole, I thought it would be funny to meet his Mennonite family all gothed out. I wore all black with platform boots, facial piercings, white foundation with tribal warpaint, and a single whiteout contact lens. I looked like a crazed Devil worshipper. His family didn't see any of that. They just knew that Bill's good friend and co-worker was visiting. The first thing out of his wife's mouth was "QUEEN!" before giving me a big hug on the porch. Their kids loved me. They weren't phased by the crazy makeup... it was like I wasn't wearing any makeup at all. I felt unconditionally accepted and loved by everyone.

We had a long talk about all sorts of things over dinner. His beautiful 17 year old daughter had hair so blonde it was nearly white and her energy was so innocent and pure... she kept wanting to hug me and ask me questions. I did not want her touching me. I felt she might be corrupted or tainted in some way. I wanted her to be protected from the darkness within me.

Later, Bill took me for a tour of his property. When we were alone he said, "You know, if you and Jessey ever wanted a nice place to live, you are always welcome to stay here with us for as long as you like." I saw the look in his eyes and was flooded with images. He was in love with me and his family would be okay with me moving in with them and sharing their lives. I was flattered and stunned.

"Unfortunately, Bill, I think I'm a bit too citified to adjust to your way of life." He nodded, looked down, looked a bit sad... and never brought it up again.

We had a great rapport. He was probably the best friend I ever had. But as much as I liked him and as generous as his offer was, I was not ready to give up partying and going to the clubs yet. Working my dream job and having my own apartment was the best time of my life. I miss it a lot.

69

I met Chris at *Muddy's*. He was the cook there and was handsome and cool. He had a shaved head and lots of muscles, claiming "Rudie" affiliation, a type of traditional skin which hated Nazis and was mostly about the music. He wore black and white checkered braces, black laces in oxblood Docs, and a nylon flight jacket covered with band and Anti-Nazi patches. I thought he was the most awesome thing ever.

We began dating. He came over to my place a few times and got along great with Jessey. He also would take me out to Rudie shows, concerts with bands like *The Specials* and *Madness*. The Nazis and SHARPs would show up at these concerts and vicious fights would ensue, usually involving knives and "smileys"... a heavy padlock swung from a bandanna or bike chain. No-one ever called the cops or waited for an ambulance... they would carry out their wounded and leave.

Since I had Anti-Nazi patches all over my flight jacket and wore a Chelsea haircut, I was frequently attacked by the Nazis at these concerts. I modified the toes of my Docs to hold 3 razor blades each, which would be invisible once I smeared them with polish, and kept a spare razor concealed in my wristband that I could palm to slash with every slap. Eventually, the doormen started checking our boots and banning spiked wristbands so it ruined our fun. No-one really got hurt that badly by the razors, they didn't cut very deep, just broke the skin.

After about a month, Chris complained of unspecified problems with his roommates and that he needed to find a new place to live quickly, but didn't have enough money for first month's rent plus a security deposit. Stupidly, I offered to let him move in with me.

The first few months, things seemed fine. On my behalf, Bill gave his recommendation that Chris be hired at the funeral home as a death certificate runner, which involved wearing a suit and driving a company car to nursing homes and hospitals to have death certificates signed by a doctor before bringing them back to be filed. It was a day job, and we didn't see each other much. He showed up for work and did his job, but Bill told me something seemed off about him and he did not like him.

Eventually, a few red flags started popping up. He would go out for hours without accounting for where or why, and hundreds of dollars we needed for bills would regularly go missing. The spirits I worked with made it obvious they hated him and made him unwelcome. At first, he would wake up and say things like, "I think your place is haunted, something kept pulling on my toes and messing with my hair." After a while, they would actually throw things at him. We would be laying on the living room floor, watching a movie on television, when a box of cereal from on top of the refrigerator in the kitchen would fly across the room and hit him in the head. That happened several times. I should've taken telekinesis as a very obvious sign that something was terribly wrong, but I was in denial and assumed that perhaps they were just being playful.

This was a very traumatic period of my life and I experienced a series of memory blackouts due to the severity of the abuse I suffered. There is a lot I am unable to recall clearly, yet other memories remain vividly clear. He began acting out towards himself first. I don't know what his issues were, but he was a skinhead in Memphis and had killed a few people there, which he never really talked about, and he had also worked on an ambulance as an EMT, but I really didn't know that much about his background at all. He was a mystery to me.

The first time he put me in the hospital he was threatening suicide with a kitchen knife, carving a series of superficial cuts on his arm which I later realized was a narcissistic manipulation technique demanding attention. When he held the knife to his throat I grabbed it and he pulled away, slicing my pinky finger to the bone. "That's pretty bad," he said, "We're going to need to take you to the ER to get that stitched up."

When we arrived at the hospital, the doctor injected my finger with Novocain to numb it and I began squishing it, looking inside the wound. It looked like chicken fat. "How did this happen?" the doctor asked. I looked over at Chris, who was standing in the corner of the room, staring at me.

"I accidentally cut myself unloading the dishwasher," I said. At that moment, I realized I was one of those weak women I hated, the ones who kept making excuses for their abuser and going back to him.

A week later, during a heated argument about unaccounted for bill money, Chris pulled his double-barreled shotgun out of the closet... but instead of threatening me, he sat down in the recliner, kicked off his shoes, placed the muzzle in his mouth, and proceeded struggling to place his sock covered toe in the trigger guard to shoot himself... but he was being really slow and inept about it, as if he was expecting me to yell "NO!" and try to stop him. It was some of the dumbest shit I'd ever seen. Then I saw Jessey in his bedroom, oblivious to what was going on, playing with a toy.

"Hold on..." I said, walking past Chris to shut the door to Jessey's room. Then I turned back to him, crossed my arms, and said, "Continue." His eyes went wide... he looked scared and confused. "I just don't want my son to see you blow your brains out," I explained. He got angry, cursed, threw the shotgun back in the closet, then stormed out, slamming the door behind him. Things took a turn for the worst after that.

70

Chris announced we were going on a camping trip in Moab. It seemed rather spontaneous and neither of us had ever been there before or even talked about going there, but it sounded awesome and I was excited to go.

We drove his beat up truck three hundred miles to get there. It was blazing hot that weekend, 115 degrees in the shade, but at least the truck had air conditioning. I was looking forward to seeing the sights and having fun... Chris didn't smile and barely talked the whole way there... he seemed oddly distracted.

We arrived in Moab and Chris had no idea where to go... he drove around aimlessly for a while before proceeding up a randomly selected Jeep trail that was little more than tire tracks in the sand. We drove way out in the middle of the badlands to set up camp.

We didn't have much in the way of equipment or supplies. We shared a nylon 2-man tent with a mesh skylight panel, and Jessey had his own pup tent. We had gotten a Chow puppy a few months earlier and had brought her with us, tying her collar to a rope attached to an eye bolt he'd hammered into the ground. It was way too hot to have a campfire, so all we brought with us to eat was stuff like chips, granola bars, and canned ravioli. A lot of horrible things happened that weekend... I got PTSD from some of those things. I have memory blackouts and cannot remember most of it. We did not drink or use any drugs, the memory loss is solely due to trauma.

I recall Chris pacing endlessly, carrying his rifle, muttering under his breath... it was an antique 9X57mm Mauser capable of dropping a buffalo with a single shot. The few times I managed to make out what he was saying it didn't make any sense... crazy talk, completely irrelevant to our current situation. He became irritable, then hostile, muttering about what a "stupid bitch" I was. I felt like I was walking on eggshells the whole weekend, being careful not to say or do anything that might make him flip out on us. I remember being really scared.

The stars were beautiful at night, and we saw lightning coming up from the ground. After a while we went to sleep. In the middle of the night the Chow woke us up with her barking. Opening our eyes, we both saw a man standing over our tent, staring down at our naked bodies through the mesh skylight. We could see him quite clearly in the moonlight. He looked like an Indian Chief, a large, older, Native American man dressed in traditional tribal garb with beads and feathers in his hair, just staring down at us, motionless, saying nothing.

We quickly threw on our clothes and rushed outside, but no-one was there. He didn't run away or hide, there was simply no place for him to go... he just vanished. We agreed it must have been a spiritual visitation of some sort and went back to sleep.

The next morning we packed up our tents and drove back down the trail to the road, driving around aimlessly once again before Chris selected another random Jeep trail nearly 50 miles away. We drove out into the badlands once again to set up camp far from everything.

Chris seemed more agitated and angry than before, muttering crazy talk under his breath, yelling that he wanted to kill us both, occasionally firing off the Mauser. He stumbled around in a daze, eyes glazed over, making absolutely no sense with his bizarre rants. He stomped to the edge of a cliff and started throwing our packs over the edge. "WHAT THE FUCK ARE YOU DOING?" I yelled, which seemed to snap him out of it. I told him that me and Jessey were going to walk all the way to Moab and take a bus home if he didn't unfuck himself. His eyes seemed to clear and he acted confused about what had just happened, peering over the cliff at where the packs had landed. Fortunately, they didn't fall very far from the edge and he was able to climb down and retrieve them.

That night the Chow's barking woke us up again. The Indian Chief was back, looking down at us through the skylight, 50 miles away from our original campsite. We both saw him very clearly. This was no dream or hallucination. As before, when we rushed out of our tent no-one was there.

We packed up everything into the truck and left the next morning. Chris insisted that Jessey could not be in the air conditioned cab with us and instead needed to ride unsecured in the back under the bed cover in 115 degree temperatures. Since he was batshit insane, armed with a high powered rifle, and had threatened to kill us both multiple times, I said nothing until after we got back onto the main road and passed back into civilization again, whereupon I began screaming that he needed to stop the truck or I would jump out... when he pulled over, I brought Jessey back up front with us and Chris seemed confused, claiming he did not remember insisting that he ride back there.

We rode the entire 300 miles back to Denver in silence. Chris seemed to be back to normal again. Being naïve and in denial, I somehow convinced myself that "the heat" had made him crazy.

I do not know who that old Indian was, but I felt absolutely nothing malevolent about him, although he enraged Chris. I got the clear impression he was watching out for me and manifested as a warning to Chris that his actions were being witnessed and any harm done to us on sacred land would have dire consequences. I am convinced that Indian spirit saved our lives. Thinking back on it, I am certain Chris had intended to murder us both in the badlands and toss our bodies off a cliff where we would never be found.

71

Chris's behavior became more erratic and crazed. He would stay out late, showing up hours after midnight, and I would wake up to him ranting accusations about how I had been cheating on him and hanging out with people I'd never heard of before. Several times I woke up to him pointing the shotgun at my face. "If you tell anyone, I'll kill you. If you try to leave me, I'll kill you," was something he started saying often, reciting almost like a mantra.

I did not know who I could talk to about this, so I tracked down a couple of his exes who agreed to speak with me. They told tales of far worse abuse than I'd yet been subject to. They also told me he had a habit of spending the bill money on prostitutes. Not respectable escorts either, but skanky crack addicted streetwalkers off Colfax. This horrified me. One of my greatest fears was that of contracting some incurable disease. I'd had a few UTIs and yeast infections since I was with him, which I had never experienced before, and was scared. I immediately got tested and was clean, but stopped having sex with him. I kept what I knew a secret. I thought he would flip out and murder me if I confronted him about what his exes had told me about his mysterious late night activities.

A few days later I heard him moving around my room and woke up. He bent over me, as if to kiss me... then bit down hard on my nose and tried to bite it off. I heard a crunch and he refused to let go, so I started screaming and hitting and finally gouged at his eyes. He got up and walked out of the apartment without another word.

The strangest thing about all this was that Chris wasn't on drugs and he wasn't a drinker. He didn't exhibit the usual signs of schizophrenia either. He was the nicest and most likeable guy ever in public, but when we were alone things would change. He would be acting fine all day, perfectly normal, then suddenly with no warning he would hit me or point a gun at me... sometimes in total silence, other times while screaming baseless accusations. I didn't see any of the typical signs of demonic possession, although that seems to be the most likely explanation for his actions. His personality would abruptly change and something else seemed to take over, his eyes would go glassy and his entire face would go slack like he was a puppet on strings, but I never saw an entity and it never identified itself to me.

Things got better for a few weeks, until one night when he took me and Jessey to the store in his truck. Afterwards, instead of going home, he began driving East... towards Eastllawn Cemetery. "Where are we going?" I asked him.

"Just for a drive," he said, in a creepy monotone, eyes forward. Something seemed off, but I said nothing. We drove up a dirt road a few miles, then into the middle of a farmer's field, out in the middle of nowhere. "Get out," he said. "Take your kid and get the fuck out." I was scared. I didn't know what to do. We were so far from anyone who could help us and he had the Mauser hanging in the gun rack, plus whatever else I didn't know about. What was he gonna do? Make us walk home? Kill us? "GET THE FUCK OUT!" he yelled. We got out.

He drove the truck away, leaving us standing in the dark... then made a U turn and floored it... directly at us. I pulled Jessey out of the way as the truck flew past. He made a few more passes, then I stumbled and was unable to get out of the way. He slammed on the brakes and the truck skidded to a halt inches away from us. Then he steered around us, made another U turn and came at us again... slamming on his brakes once more. I had twisted my ankle and was crying. He opened the door. "Get in the truck."

"No."

"GET IN THE FUCKING TRUCK!" he yelled, reaching for the
Mauser. We got in the truck. He drove us home like nothing
had happened and never spoke of the matter again.

A week later he came home on his lunch break, as he often did. I
had gone out that morning for breakfast with the new girl working
at the mortuary and for some reason that enraged him. While I
was ironing his work shirts he stormed up yelling accusations that
I had been cheating on him with the new female coworker... then
he punched me in the face as hard as he could.

I had never been punched in the face before and always
wondered what it felt like. I had been slapped plenty of times,
elbowed in the face at shows, punched in places other than the
face. This was a new and shocking experience for me... and at
that moment I was Enlightened. I smiled... then I punched him
back... with the hot iron in my hand. He dropped to the ground.

"Pack your shit and get the fuck out," I said.

"But I don't have anywhere to go!" he whined.

"I don't care if you die in the gutter, motherfucker! Get the fuck
out!" He did.

He went back to finish up his shift at work, while I collected all his
belongings and put them on the curb. Then I called the funeral
home to talk to him. "All your shit is on the curb behind the
apartment. If you try to come inside I'm calling the cops." I hung
up.

My downstairs neighbor was a retired cop, and he agreed to keep
an eye on my place and make sure Chris didn't try to break in.
He showed up later, yelling from the curb to let him back in, but I
ignored him. He loaded his shit into the back of his truck and
drove away. He was a no show at work the following day and
never showed up there again.

When Bill saw my black eye he asked me what happened, and I lied and told him I'd gotten in a fight with some girl at a bar. "Is that really what happened?" he asked. I didn't answer. I couldn't look him in the eye. He knew what had happened and was really upset. I felt like such a piece of shit.

A few months later I got a letter in the mail from Chris. He had joined the Army because he had burned all his bridges and run out of options. "I still love you," he wrote. He said other lies as well. I wrote back, telling him never to contact me again.

72

Because Chris had cleaned out all my savings before he left, I was unable to pay rent on time and was served with eviction papers. I needed to find a new place to live in a hurry. Moving back with Karen was not an option, and I had no intention of taking Bill up on his generous offer of being his live in concubine. I called my friend Mo who I knew from *Muddy's* and the clubs. Next to Bill, she was probably my best friend in the world. She agreed to rent a bedroom to me for $300 a month.

I needed to discard most of my belongings, keeping my couch that turned into a foldout bed, dresser, and altar as well as Jessey's bed. Mo had recently had a baby and was not working, welfare paid the rent and provided her food stamps. The $300 I gave her was some extra spending money. We had the entire first floor of an old house in Park Hill on MLK Boulevard, with another tenant renting the upstairs.

Mo was a slight woman, short and frail with red hair and freckles. She was always complaining of one health problem or another, I think she was a bit of a hypochondriac. She was a Wiccan who claimed to practice some sort of Celtic *Fae* based magick and took it somewhat seriously, always saging the house, tracing wards over the doors, celebrating the traditional holidays, and practicing herbology. She understood that my magick was darker than hers but seemed to have no issues with that.

Things went great for a while, but then she began sleeping all the time and her toddler would crawl all over the house unsupervised, chewing on electrical wires and torturing the cat. This affected my sleep because I felt obligated to watch him after coming home from work and finding him loose. Then I would need to pick up Jessey from daycare before going to work again. I was lucky to manage an hour nap a day, doing most of my sleeping on the weekends.

Soon, our little house became very crowded. First, she began dating this creep named James, who I was unfailingly polite to but he never liked me. He had some tech job making good money. Within a month he moved in. Then, her two teenaged sons who had been living with her ex moved in, a 15 year old and an 18 year old... and the older boy brought along his 16 year old girlfriend, whom Mo unofficially adopted as her "future daughter in law."

The teenagers were loud, rude, and disrespectful, with the girl being worst of all. Occasionally Serpent or another of my male friends would visit and she would obnoxiously begin making out with her boyfriend on the couch... then lock eyes with my friend while spreading her legs to show she wasn't wearing any panties under her miniskirt, flashing her shaved coochie hoping for a reaction. Usually they would just get up and walk out. Needless to say, all this disruption deprived me of even more sleep.

Within a month, Mo suddenly claimed I "hadn't been paying for utilities or food" and had been "costing them a lot of money." This made absolutely no sense at all, as I always paid my rent nearly a week early, which was all inclusive, and bought most of the food in the house myself. I also rarely ate at home. Then she proceeded to blame me for eating all the food in the fridge and trashing the kitchen and filling the sink with dirty dishes, but that was her teenagers, not me, and I told her so before leaving for work.

When I returned the next morning, all my furniture was dumped in the alley behind the house, in the ghetto, for anyone to come by and pick through. Jessey was sitting on the back steps crying. They had changed the locks so my key no longer worked and refused to answer the door. I took Jessey to a neighbor we knew to use their phone to call the cops. When the Denver Police arrived, Mo refused to answer the door for them too. They told me that "possession is 9/10ths of the law" and since I was not on the lease I had no rights and was trespassing.

Mo had taken all the herbs, crystals, and ritual tools from my altar as well as my journal, book of shadows, the manuscript of the novel I was writing, and over a dozen magick books. She also had taken all my porcelain figurines from Germany and half of my clothes which didn't even fit her but would've fit the girl. Furthermore, all of Jessey's toys, including the brand new Xbox 360 I'd bought him for Christmas, she kept. This was later confirmed by a mutual friend who told me she saw the figurines in a display case in her livingroom and the teenagers were playing the Xbox. All of my bones were missing as well... except for Elizabeth, who had insisted that I wear her around my neck that day.

Having no place to go, I called my friend Tab, who could not let me stay with him, but loaded my furniture into his truck to keep in his storage unit until I got settled. Moving back in with Karen was not an option, and Bill would expect too much if I asked to stay with him, so me and Jessey lived in the Cavalier for a couple of months, occasionally couch surfing for a few days here and there. I would often take him to work with me, although it wasn't allowed. Bill said he would pretend he didn't see anything, and we would unroll a sleeping bag under one of the desks in the office for Jessey to sleep. Bill always let me leave an hour before the office staff arrived, but one day someone showed up an hour early and saw him and it was a huge deal and I was written up.

About a month later I was driving past Mo's house and she was walking outside. She spotted me and began running after my car, waving her arms yelling for me to pull over, which I did, rolling down the passenger window.

"Queen! I am so sorry about what happened! It wasn't my fault! James changed the locks and threw your stuff out! He made me go along with it, I didn't want to! The cancer came back! I've been so sick!" I looked at her. She was disheveled and jaundiced, her skin and eyes a sickly shade of yellow. If she was lying about being sick before, she certainly wasn't now.

"That is your Karma, all of it at once... you deserve everything that is about to happen to you." I smiled as her eyes widened in horror. I drove off, leaving her standing there in shock.

I do not know whatever happened to Mo. Everyone in the scene knew her, but she dropped out and vanished. A month later, the downstairs of her house was vacant and a "for rent" sign was on the front lawn. I tried tracking her down, but I never even knew her real name, just her scene name which was some shit like "Morgana LaFey." It's a shame she disappeared. I really wanted to bash her fucking head to pieces with a hammer.

73

Shortly thereafter, our funeral home was acquired by the corporate mortuary giant *SCI*, who immediately replaced all the administrators and fired more than half our staff, including most of our best people, to "cut costs." I was also put on the chopping block. The written reprimand from 2 months earlier about letting Jessey sleep in the office was cited as well as a series of baseless accusations that I "looked like a Devil worshipper" and "someone said she saw you trimming a body's fingernails and putting the clippings in your pocket."

Bill talked to the owners and stated that I was the best desairologist and hardest worker he'd ever known, and if I was let go he would quit. I was let go anyway. The biggest reason seemed to be that I was two months away from qualifying for an all expenses paid 2 year scholarship to *Mortuary Sciences School* in Texas... which *SCI* would be obligated to pay for, per my contract.

I never stole from my employer, and certainly never mishandled any of the remains in any way. But after they told me I was gone at the end of the week I did steal a really cool embalming jacket that was covered in stains and a couple packs of suturing needles. I loved that jacket and wore it everywhere for a while. I don't know whatever happened to it.

I was offered a job as a desairologist at Fairmount, but it was only "on call" as needed, which did not pay the bills, so I was soon forced to wait tables at a greasy spoon called *The White Spot* on Broadway to survive. Bill quit, as he said he would, and was immediately hired at a small family owned funeral home closer to where he lived.

I applied at a dozen other funeral homes and never even got a call back, which made no sense to me given my references. Much later, I discovered that *SCI* had blacklisted me, and they run over 95% of the funeral homes in Colorado. Another dream crushed.

74

I made less than minimum wage as a "tipped employee" at *The White Spot,* but made great tips. Soon, I was able to afford a new apartment at "The Bahamas" in Aurora, off Colfax near Jamaica.

It was set up like a hotel, a horseshoe shaped 4 story building with doors on the landings, surrounding a giant pool. There also was a tall metal fence with a security gate that required an access code to open. It was one of the nicest apartment buildings I'd ever seen. The landlord was a gamer geek who had an entire room in his unit devoted to playing a SciFi boardgame called *BattleTech,* which used hundreds of lead figurines of fighters in robotic battle armor bristling with weapons. It was awesome. I would sit in his apartment playing the angry robot game for hours, even buying and painting my own figurines. I had a lot of fun doing that.

Ozzy died shortly after I moved in. The transmission went out and I couldn't afford to have it fixed... I couldn't even afford to have it towed. I just took off the plates, filled a couple bags with assorted items, said goodbye, and walked away, leaving it on the side of the road. I could not afford another car either. I started taking the bus everywhere.

Around this time, I began spending time with a guy I knew from the club named Drake. I'd known him for a few years prior to that. He seemed like a cool guy, and was into chaos magick and BDSM, both of which I had a strong interest in. He also had some serious connections with a few occult groups like Temple of Set and an esoteric Masonic splinter group.

We began doing magick together. Mostly just basic rituals to build strength or request guidance. A few of these rituals involved bloodletting with razors to draw sigils. Once, while we were simultaneously cutting each other, he sliced too deeply and my arm opened up, exposing my bicep muscle. It didn't hurt. I just poured alcohol over it and slapped on some duct tape and it was fine.

He presented himself as a Dom and had a few whips which he was very skilled with. I had always wanted to experience a proper flogging and he used a cat-o-nine tails a few times, which I enjoyed. It was a transcendental experience. The bliss of the endorphins drove me into a deep meditative state. I loved it.

We only had sex once. I consented to it, but made it very clear that this was only recreational and I did not want a boyfriend or any sort of romantic relationship, which he agreed to. I was blindfolded and bound. It was an awful experience. I didn't even get off once, and then he tried going anal without lube and tore my ass, making me cry. I told him to stop and he did. I was really pissed off at him for weeks and we never had sex again.

The next time he came over he brought the bullwhip. "Everyone is afraid of the bullwhip, it's too extreme for them... would you like to experience this?"

"Yes."

It was incredibly painful, but I did not cry out and he hit me again, harder... then again.

"You're bleeding... do you want me to continue?"

"Yes." The pain was worse than anything I'd ever experienced, aside from childbirth. It was sharp and overwhelming. I was crying.

I needed to cry, a lot of things that had been locked away were suddenly released... and the pain stopped. I opened my eyes and realized I was standing in the corner, facing myself, watching myself be whipped. I had projected out of my body again. A few minutes later he coiled the bullwhip up and put it away. Instantly, I was back in my body. It hurt all over. I was shaking. "Are you alright?" he asked.

"I think so." I had five long gashes across my back, which I rinsed off in the shower and splashed with alcohol. I wasn't able to wear a bra for weeks.

After this, I noticed a change in Drake. Just a few red flags here and there at first. He started showing up at my apartment unannounced, and I'd heard from people I knew at the club that he'd been referring to me as his girlfriend. I called him on it and he apologized and said he'd stop.

He became a lot more intense, almost obsessive with me. His whole attitude changed, like something inside had shifted. He stopped ordering mixers at the club, drinking only red wine instead. The expression on his face was different too. He smiled all the time now, but not a happy smile, more of a cruel and condescending one... almost like a *smirk*.

75

I met Moonflower at the club. She would wear denim coveralls instead of goth clothes. She was a heavyset woman with long red hair.

Moonflower was a mathematical genius who was fascinated with Numerology and Astrology... but she took it deeper than anyone I ever knew. Most people use your given name to do a numerological reading. She used an astrological chart... a computer generated chart that was over 25 pages long. Your time of birth, rising sign, and the apogee and degree of every planet and the moon was formulated to create a series of numbers, that then was changed to letters, which formed a word.

My numbers spelled out: **UZAZIEL**.

"That is who you are," she told me. "That is your True Name."

I did weeks of research on Uzaziel, but there wasn't much out there to find, aside from a few obscure references. Apparently, Uzaziel was an Angel, but had fallen with Lucifer and many others, a third of the Host, nearly 700,000 others. Uzaziel had some rank, but which rank was unclear. He didn't appear to be particularly evil either. Indeed, some books showed a solid connection with the Archangel Usiel, in some cases claiming it was an alternate spelling, of which there were several.

I meditated on Uzaziel frequently, often spending hours staring into an antique silver backed mirror by candlelight. Eventually, the face appeared to me, the white face like carved marble, with sharp features... but the eyes were not black... they were bright and shining.

"Hello," the voice in my head spoke. I got the strong impression that there was some sort of rule which prevented it from revealing itself to me before I went looking for it. "I am older than the Universe," it told me. It told me many other things over the years. Unfortunately, I have forgotten most of them. I never thought to keep notes. I was unsure if what I was experiencing was real or some sort of psychotic hallucination. I told no-one.

76

I waited tables full-time on the graveyard shift at *The White Spot* at 8ᵗʰ and Broadway. Everyone called it "The Wet Spot." The manager was gay, and the place was extremely popular with the LGBT community, especially the drag queens. We had a very diverse clientele, being open 24 hours in the club district, but during the day it was mostly old people and businessmen. I much preferred graveyard shift, and the drag queens were the best tippers.

Every Saturday night around 2 AM, a dozen drag queens would show up and order about two hundred dollars worth of food, run us ragged for a couple of hours asking for refills, appetizers, and desserts but then after they paid the bill would only leave a dollar! This really pissed us off, but we continued to be civil to them and never said a word about it. All of us complained about them. Usually only the church ladies on Sunday morning pulled shit like that, it was unheard of for drag queens to do it. Then one night the head waitress saw each of them throw down a five or ten dollar bill as a tip... about $80 worth of tips... and they gradually got up to leave one by one... then the last one remaining pocketed the whole wad of bills and threw down a dollar! That motherfucker!

The next time they came in, while the thief was in the restroom the head waitress walked over and told everyone at the table that their friend had been stealing the tip money and only leaving the waitress a dollar. They collectively let out a gasp... a few of them teared up, apologizing profusely. They were mortified by what he had done. When he returned to the table they all glared at him in silence. He knew he fucked up. "The waitress told us you've been pocketing our tips. You can't sit with us anymore, and you're out of the show."

We did not see him for a few weeks. The next time he came in, he was in drag with his usual wig and makeup, but instead of a grand sequined gown he was wearing a rather conservative skirt and sweater. He was with two other people in drag whom we had not seen before. He ordered the Salisbury steak with mashed potatoes and gravy... and he was sitting at my table.

I told the cooks the creep who had stolen the tips just ordered a Salisbury steak. They all knew what he had done and were waiting for him to come back. This went way beyond the "special sauce" in that movie *Waiting*... they did shit to that man's steak that made me gag. I stood in the doorway with my arms crossed and watched it all.

First, someone tugged down his pants and wiped his ass with the raw steak, before using tongs to dip it into the grease trap in the floor, then tossing it under the stove where they never swept and pulling it out... he brushed off some of the debris with a dirty rag before adding a spice rub. Another cook blew his nose in the frying pan before adding butter to it. The third cook rubbed a piece of Italian bread all over his armpits, crotch, and ass before adding butter and garlic powder and placing it in the toaster. A lot of snot and loogies went into those mashed potatoes before they added extra butter and black pepper. Someone poured gravy into a cup, gargled with it, then spit it over the potatoes. Dinner was served!

Everyone on staff knew we had given his food the special treatment, but had no idea how far they'd taken it... I am not sure what combination of drugs the cooks were on that night, but cocaine was always a factor. Anyway, all eyes were on me as I very professionally set the plate in front of him like we hadn't just committed multiple crimes and health code violations upon his entrée. He was all smiles as he cut a piece of that abomination and ate it, chewing blissfully. He ate the whole thing, every bit of snotfilled taters and the entire piece of jock strap infused garlic bread. He practically licked the plate clean. Then, when paying the bill, he beamed up at me and stated it was the best meal he'd ever ate and thanked me.

When he got up to leave, he left me a dollar.

We laughed our asses off over that befouled Salisbury steak all week. I never told the other girls what I saw the cooks do... they thought they only wiped it on the floor and spit on it, and I felt it was best not to shatter any illusion of sanity in the kitchen.

A couple weeks later he returned, and ordered the same meal... then complained it "wasn't as good as last time."

77

Drake started acting differently. He began doing small things to annoy or upset me, then would try gaslighting me about it. One thing he started doing was grabbing the sensitive hairs at the nape of my neck and yanking on them. When I yelled and cursed at him, he would act surprised and say, "You always used to like that," but this was a new thing he'd never done before, and he kept doing it. Another thing he started doing was keeping his Bic lighter lit until the metal heated up, then pressing it against my arm to burn me. He acted like it was some sort of harmless practical joke. He began drinking more red wine, and wore that smirk constantly now.

One night at club, he introduced me to a friend of his he knew from the Temple of Set, a young guy with a barrel chest, shaved head, and goatee. I had run into this guy at *Muddy's* about a month before and he was a real dick. We had been discussing spiritual matters when he became all condescending and snide, borderline hostile. I did not think much of him or the Temple of Set... the Denver Temple all liked to boast about their powers of psychic vampirism and how they could attack enemies in their dreams. It was all like a game to them.

He recognized me as soon as we were introduced, and was abrupt and curt before walking away. "What happened?" Drake asked, seemingly upset. "I'd thought you two would have lots in common!" I told him the circumstances of our earlier meeting and he nodded and said no more.

That night I began having a series of recurring dreams in which the bald creep was chasing me up a spiral staircase in an ivory tower. The tower was similar to the one we saw in my guided meditation days and never reached, but it was in the middle of a desert and the stairs seemed to go on forever. The banisters and caps on the corners of each stair were polished gold.

Somehow, I knew that I needed to reach the pinnacle of the tower if I wanted to live, but he kept grabbing me by an ankle and dragging me down, whereupon I would awaken. The third night, I got pissed off. I wasn't going to run from this creep anymore. I stopped, spun around, and kicked him up under the jaw as hard as I could. Both his feet lifted off the stairs and he fell backwards, seemingly unconscious, tumbling all the way down the stairs to the bottom. I continued up the stairs, which ended at a windowless landing. I faced a pure white door with a golden knob. Unhesitating, I reached forward to claim my prize. The moment before touching the doorknob I woke up.

I told Drake about this and he laughed, thinking it was funny. That weekend he introduced me to another friend of his, Justine, also from the Temple of Set. Supposedly she was their High Priestess in Denver. She acted like she was so superior to me, like her shit didn't stink, a real nasty bitch for someone so young and pretty. She barely deigned to speak a few words to me before abruptly turning and walking away.

A few nights later, she came after me on the Astral to attack me in a dream... but I was not dreaming... I was my Other, in my angelic aspect. Clipboard in hand, I stood in the Realm of the Dead performing my assigned task, the sorting of souls, sending each to their proper realm. I was not Queen here, I was **UZAZIEL**... and she was way out of her league... the poor thing didn't even know where she was!

She fumbled with an object in her hands, a powerful weapon she'd been entrusted with that she had no idea how to use. She extended it towards me, chanting some sort of mantra... but she was holding it wrong. I snatched it away and looked down at it. It was a metallic cone, sort of like a brushed steel party hat. The big end was crimped like a shotgun shell and a red tassel hung from the point.

"You do not know how to use this. Here, let me show you." Uzaziel said, then began chanting in tongues... I had no idea what was being said... before turning the big end towards her and ripping out the tassel like an oversized party popper. There was no noise or flash and I didn't see anything come out the other end, but she flew backwards and rapidly began fading away. Several of the souls flew after her, intent on attacking her for her transgression. Then I woke up, still chanting words I did not understand.

The next day, Drake unexpectedly asked what had happened between me and Justine. I didn't reveal many details, just that she had tried attacking me in a dream and I fought her off. "Well, she is absolutely terrified of you now. She can't even say your name!" And then he laughed, a cackling maniacal laugh I began to know very well.

78

One night Drake brought home a stack of typed papers outlining a number of Masonic Illuminati type protocols... everything was very structured and precise. I had never seen anything like it before. It was all rather impressive.

"One of my friend's family is deep into the Masons, very high level shit, and he's very interested in meeting you. He wants to start his own group and asked me to have you read through this information to see if you agreed with it and if it was something you might be interested in." I told him I was very interested and would be glad to meet him.

About a week later he brought the guy over to my apartment. He was a Chad in a polo shirt who was impeccably groomed... he looked like a Ken doll... since I cannot recall his name I'll just call him Ken.

We had a few beers and he asked me a number of questions about my heritage. He seemed relieved when he heard that I was adopted and was not half black, then got excited when I told him that both my parents were German and my father was a German Army officer. Then we spent most of the night talking about our beliefs and personal philosophies.

"I want to form a group called The Order of the Morning Star based on these beliefs. Would you be willing to tone down your appearance and exuberance a bit so you could act as the spokesperson for our group?" The rich boy with the fancy car and millionaire parents just asked if I wanted to be a cult leader.

"Alright."

Unfortunately, things went sideways immediately afterwards and that was yet another opportunity lost...

79

I began working part-time at *Hot Topic* in Westminster as a sales associate before quickly being promoted to keyholder, then offered a position as full-time assistant manager. I quit waiting tables altogether to start fresh with a new career. I loved the product and my coworkers and the customers. This was back when they were still cool, before they sold out and went mainstream Goth Lite. It was a much needed change.

I had distanced myself from Drake, but he kept showing up unannounced at my work, telling me about new sex toys he had bought and asking when we could use them. "Never," I told him, "I'm never having sex with you again." Then he would pout and leave... but would be back again in a week, saying the same stupid shit.

Another creepy thing was that he was having a friend of his keep tabs on me, a weirdo with hair like a Brillo pad. He had introduced me to him and his wife at the club months earlier, and often they would show up at *The White Spot,* but never sat in my section. A few times other waitresses told me a couple had been in on my night off and was asking about me, saying they were friends who wanted to say hi. When I asked them to describe them they always said, "Well, it was a white guy with a strawberry blonde afro." And now they were randomly showing up at *Hot Topic,* lurking around the corners, never buying anything, then sneaking out without a word.

Aside from the relentless stalking, working at *Hot Topic* was great. I loved interacting with the customers. I would not sell anyone a corset until I was satisfied that it fit properly and they were able to put it on by themselves. I also would refuse to sell poseurs T-shirts to bands I liked unless they could prove they were a fan by reciting the lyrics to one of their songs. "I am doing this for your own good," I would tell them, "You don't want to wear that on the 16th Street Mall and get called out for it." Not too many years ago, my friends would've beat their ass, cut off their silly green Mohawk, and stole their Docs for being a poseur. I was doing them a favor.

I loved my job.

80

Drake became insanely obsessed with me and had given up on calling my number a hundred times a day or ringing my buzzer for hours. Now he was climbing an 8 foot tall metal fence in the middle of the night to pound on my door and try peeking in my windows. I never answered.

Due to the blood magick and that one regrettable sexual encounter, I had a psionic link with Drake, and I always knew when he was coming. I would feel his presence or see a vision of his face as he was driving to my apartment building... and within 20 minutes he'd be pounding on the door. He never yelled so the neighbors minded their business, and I never called the cops because I'm no snitch. I would just let him wear himself out pounding on the door, then he would go home.

One night my friend Tad was hanging out late, watching movies, when I got another vision and immediately went tense. "Drake is coming!" I said.

"How do you know?" he asked, skeptically. I explained how I saw a vision of his face, which always meant he was on his way and would be there soon. He scoffed, convinced I was delusional and causing drama for attention. He was not spiritually inclined at all, which was a big reason why we weren't dating.

Twenty minutes later, Drake was pounding on the door. Tad insisted on opening the door, but I told him I would. I finally answered the door, stepping out onto the balcony and closing it behind me.

"Why are you pounding on my door, Drake?"

"You never answer your phone anymore! What do you expect me to do?"

"You can't keep jumping my fence to harass me. I live in a secure building for a reason, and if I don't answer my phone or my doorbell, that means I don't want to be disturbed, and you need to respect that."

He pouted for a few minutes, and complained that I had another guy there, before storming off. If Tad wasn't there I never would've opened the door. He was batshit crazy at this point and I did not trust him at all. He occasionally showed up at *Hot Topic* and continued to stalk me randomly for years at a series of addresses. He sent me letters flat out stating he intended to abduct me so I would be "his forever." Over 20 years later, he continues to stalk me on social media and even though he lives over a hundred miles from Denver and I rarely pass through town anymore, I'm still worried about running into him at an event.

Fuck you, Drake.

81

Courtney was one of my customers at *Hot Topic*, a short dumpy lesbian with the physique of a beach ball, but she was super nice and had a lot of cool interests. We began hanging out.

She introduced me to Rave culture, new genres of music, and X. It was a whole new world for me to explore. She fancied herself a DJ and sometimes would play house parties on borrowed equipment. She only played Techno: mostly Trance, mixed with House and Jungle. It had some cool beats but wasn't quite heavy enough for me.

Eventually, I moved into her place at 8th and Clarkson in Capitol Hill with Jessey. She was a great roommate, but sometimes while we were rolling she would try making an awkward pass at me, begging me to take her virginity. I wasn't attracted to her at all and just wanted to remain friends. Eventually, I found out she'd been telling everyone in the scene we were a couple anyway. That should've been my first red flag that she was batshit crazy. There would be others.

I began learning how to spin, scratch and mix, but most of the music I wanted to use was unavailable on vinyl or very hard to find. Eventually I was able to acquire some suitable records: *NIN, Ministry, Skinny Puppy, Wumpscut.* Industrial mixed well with Trance, and people at the parties we played loved it. Courtney would dress the part of a Techno DJ, with the pastel colors, candy beads, visor, and hoody. I would wear all black, with latex pants, bondage belt, platform boots, and black beads. Goth ravers would call themselves "gravers" but I felt I was doing something completely different with the Industrial mixes, so I made up the label "Rivet Raver" which seems to have stuck.

In addition to house parties, we occasionally DJed at *3 Kings* back when it used to be a lesbian bar, and performed at events held to benefit *Rainbow Alley,* which was a homeless shelter similar to *Urban Peak* but exclusively for LGBT youth. We became so popular *Westword* readers nominated us for "Best Female Tag Team DJ" and we were invited to a competition, but life got in the way and we never made it that far before shit went sideways.

Rave culture had a huge impact on my life, and continues to influence my dress and makeup to this day. I still love glitter, colorful hair extensions, and glow sticks.

82

I loved rolling on X. It was my favorite drug, but it would dehydrate you and make you grind your teeth, which is why those stupid pacifiers became associated with Rave culture... and yes, I had one too... we all did.

I had a lot of really cool experiences on X, but the most significant one was when I somehow accessed a time portal.

We had been rolling hard at a Rave in the warehouse district, before going to an alcohol free afterparty at another warehouse. I was drinking fruit juice while sitting on a subwoofer speaker, when suddenly I was seized by a wave of nausea and vomited on the floor. I had never puked from rolling before and had no idea how it would effect me. We went outside to get some air. I walked across the street to sit on the steps of yet another warehouse and closed my eyes.

When I reopened them, something was peculiar about my vision... an octagonal grid was in front of my face, almost like looking through a chickenwire fence. It was so real I put out my hands to push it away but nothing was there.

There was a crowd of people out in the street, busily walking to and fro, but they were all dressed like they were from the 1920s, with women dressed like Flappers and men wearing suits with hats. It seemed almost like watching an old film, but it was in full color and they were 3D like they were really there. It was as if a window had opened up into the past, but it was completely silent. I would be inclined to suspect that this is what parapsychologists refer to as an "imprint," except that a few of them turned to look directly at me and seemed to notice me.

"Holy shit, are you seeing this? Do you see all these people?" I asked Courtney.

"There are no people there, the street is empty." Courtney said.

I'd thought we'd been out there for maybe 20 minutes and I'd been watching these people almost the entire time, then they faded away and the grid vanished so we went back inside to find that over 2 hours had passed and they were packing up and shutting down.

We took a bus home. It was a very unique experience, especially that odd multifaceted grid across my field of vision. I'd never had a similar experience before or since.

83

Sometimes when we were rolling, we would take the bus to Walmart to hug fluffy pillows and play with the stuffed animals, because tactile sensations are a huge part of the XTC experience.

It was shortly before Easter, so there was a huge display of stuffed Easter Bunnies. For some reason I never liked rabbits and never wanted a stuffed bunny, but we looked at them anyway because we were high.

All the bunnies looked exactly the same... the same smile, the same pose, the same ears, the same grotesque pastel sea foam color... happy happy bunnies with wide eyes and outstretched arms... all except for one.

One bunny was off to the side, all by himself, about two feet away from the others on the bottom shelf. His ears were floppy, his eyes were narrowed under bushy brows, his shoulders were puffed up with hands on his hips, and he was not smiling. A Chinese sweatshop worker had sewn his mouth upside-down so he was scowling. He sat alone, glaring at that mass of stupid smiling bunnies. I burst out laughing.

"I love you," I told him. "You are coming home with me." He was twelve dollars and ninety nine cents.

I immediately dubbed him, "Mister Meanface" and made him a choker with his name spelled out with beads. I took him to a bunch of Raves, a couple Gatherings, and PRIDE Fest. I would either carry him in my arms or on my shoulders. Everyone loved the mean looking bunny.

He has slept on my bed in every apartment and ridden in the sleeper compartment of every truck. He is sitting in the back of my new Kenworth right now, listening to music. I have had him for 20 years.

Mister Meanface has seen a lot of shit.

84

As much as I loved working at *Hot Topic*, it was a long way to go on the bus everyday, with several transfers. I began looking for something closer to Capitol Hill, and eventually heard that *Fascinations* at Alameda and Colorado was hiring, so I submitted my resume to the sex toy store.

When I sat down for my interview, before it even started, I was staring at this guy while he shuffled through my resume, when suddenly, very loudly and clearly, I heard inside my head, "I am going to spend a very long time with this person." Where the fuck did THAT come from? I ignored it as it made absolutely no sense. I knew nothing about this person, I didn't even know if I had the job, but I *did* know I had a very strict policy of never dating coworkers.

I was hired, had limited contact with that manager, and promptly forgot about that weird auditory hallucination. I loved working at *Fascinations*. It was a great place to work. My coworkers were like family, and the whole atmosphere was very liberating and open. I was practically a relationship counselor to some new customers who would timidly request information regarding our products, later returning to happily proclaim that my advice had helped to improve their sex lives.

One of my favorite things about *Fascinations* was our store's shoplifting policy. Nearly every retail store in Denver had a strict no chase policy, due to liability and lawsuits... you were not allowed to confront or touch a shoplifter and were expected to let them go. At *Fascinations* we had a big black double-dong that was two feet long and three inches in diameter that we would beat the shit out of people with until they dropped what they stole. We never made an arrest and they never filed a police complaint, but after we beat someone with the double-dong they never came back. It was heavy and it hurt, leaving a huge dick shaped bruise wherever it hit.

A friend had gifted me a beat up Honda CRX which I loved... not quite as fast as Tad's RX7 Twin Turbo, but plenty quick enough to smoke the Chads in their stupid Mustangs and Camaros at stoplights.

I'd been a fan of the band *Insane Clown Posse* for years. I know, a lot of people hate Juggalos, and often for good cause because most Juggalos are stupid dipshits, but their music was like nothing else I'd ever heard. It was empowering to me, and helped me to recover after the abuse of Chris and the stalking of Drake. I listened to them a lot, and had a "Hatchetman" decal in the back window of my CRX.

One day, these two chicks came into *Fascinations* and one of them started yelling, "Hey! Who here has the Hatchetman on their car?"

"That would be me," I said.

"OH MY GOD! You're so cool and you look awesome and you work in a porn store! I just won a settlement and we're going to The Gathering and you *have* to come with us! We'll pay for your plane ticket and the suite and everything!" The 2^{d} *Annual Gathering of the Juggalos* was being held in Ohio and I'd just been offered an all expenses paid vacation by two complete strangers. What could I possibly say to that?

"Alright."

Courtney had a jealous fit when she heard two girls offered to take me on vacation and she wasn't invited. She couldn't understand why she couldn't go too. "Well, I was the only person they invited, and they don't know you and are paying my way, so I can't expect them to pay your way too." This should've been my second big red flag.

85

The Gathering was a fucking hellhole, packed in that shitty Toledo convention center, but I had a great time anyway and it was a positive lifechanging experience. From that point forth, I became a Juggalo (NOT a fucking "juggalette"), and began getting the tattoos and wearing the gear like a dedicated fan. We were a motherfucking *Family.*

Many people hate *ICP* because it is Rap-Rock with Horrorcore lyrics and the average Juggalo is a dysfunctional dipshit... but there is a LOT you do not know about them... case in point: the story behind the *2ᵈ GOTJ* in motherfucking Toledo.

Anyway, a 15 year old boy was arrested for walking down the street in an *ICP* shirt and accused of "displaying gang paraphernalia" because apparently Juggalos are allegedly a gang (this was a decade before the FBI's misguided "hybrid gang" designation). A bunch of *ICP* fans wrote letters to *Psychopathic Records* about his upcoming court case and, completely unannounced, the band walked into the courtroom on that date with a team of attorneys who completely destroyed the City of Toledo's case... but instead of suing them for millions of dollars, they demanded the use of the *Seagate Convention Center* as well as the surrounding blocks being shut down to traffic, because goddamn, they were having a motherfucking Juggalo Convention right in the middle of their city to show Toledo exactly who the Juggalos were and what they were about.

The city agreed to the terms, but the Toledo PD were outraged and decided to make things as difficult for the fans as possible.

Approximately 200,000 fans showed up to represent in Toledo... way more than *Seagate* was equipped to handle. They were all permitted inside to attend the events (in flagrant violation of Fire Code), but there were not nearly enough hotel rooms and the only food available was pizza. Most of us were forced to walk through a phalanx of police officers, including officers mounted on horseback, in order to get to our hotels or eat at McDonalds. They even had snipers on the roofs pointing rifles at us.

The mounted officers would move forward, pressing a Juggalo against the wall with the horse's head... and if he tried to push the horse away he'd be arrested for "assaulting a police animal." We saw this happen about 20 times during the 3 day Gathering. Everyone who went outside the convention center was subject to random harassment and arbitrary arrest... which of course included a patdown search as well as logging their name and address. Over a thousand Juggalos were detained without cause, searched, and immediately released. The newspaper claimed that less than a hundred were arrested "only for major crimes like drug dealing... and one Juggalo even punched a police horse!" Yeah.

The 3 day Gathering had continuous events scheduled: games, concerts, presentations, seminars, and Q&A sessions with the band who would freely discuss business ventures like side projects and new bands they were considering promoting... Psychopathic Records would not sign a new band to their label unless they agreed to perform at a Gathering so the fans could vote on whether they were awesome or sucked. We all felt included in something important. For many Juggalos, the Gathering was the only time in their life they felt important and validated. For some, this was the only family they ever had, the first time anyone ever told them "I love you brother, good to see you." Juggalo culture is almost like a mutual aid society... the band raises millions for charity, much of which goes to Juggalos who cannot afford to pay medical bills. *ICP* has done a ton of good works that no-one ever recognizes or acknowledges... they certainly don't widely advertise it like the motorcycle clubs do.

Insane Clown Posse has always had their fans' backs and put them first. Always. And that is why they will always have my love and respect.

86

Aside from my entry medallion, my most prized possession from that Gathering was an oversized red jersey that said JUGGALO on the back. One night after work at about 2 AM, I was sitting at a bus stop at Colfax and Colorado, listening to music on my headphones, when I noticed a shiny black Lincoln with dark tinted windows and 22" chrome wire rims roll past...

A few minutes later, it rolled past again, much slower, with the passenger window partially cracked...

They drove around the block and came by a third time... slowing down to a near stop... the window rolled down further and a big black hand with a big diamond ring pointed a finger at me with its thumb cocked back like the hammer of a gun. Suddenly I realized I was sitting on a bench wearing a bright red jersey *in a Crip hood!* I quickly held up both my hands and mouthed the word NOOOOOOOO while stripping down to my sports bra. They drove off and the RTD bus picked me up shortly thereafter.

I felt really stupid. I hadn't been in deep street for so many years niggaz done caught me slippin, yo, an wuz 'bout ta be all like, bap bap bap! I stopped wearing my red jersey anywhere other than The Gathering from that day forward.

87

On New Years Eve of the new Millennium, there was a *Cramps* concert at the *Ogden* on Colfax. I was invited to go with a few friends.

Security was very tight and they were wanding people at the door, making ticket holders bring pocket knives, spiked wristbands, and even wallet chains back to their cars... but as soon as we stepped into the theater ushers were randomly handing out full sized glass bottles of champagne!

We split up, some of us going to the bar, most of us going down to the pit, leaving me alone with this pretty little girl I barely knew. We were standing on the first level above the floor, leaning against the railing, watching the show.

About an hour into the concert, a group of about a half dozen Nazi skins noticed my pretty friend and decided to rape her. Back in the 90s, girls got gang raped at concerts regularly in Denver, right in front of everyone, and no-one ever did shit and no-one ever was arrested or charged because "She shouldn't have worn that dress to that concert if she didn't want some dick."

The Nazis grabbed her by the ankles and tried pulling her under the railing down to the floor. She started screaming and clutched the railing in a death hold, and I started kicking motherfuckers in the face with my Docs. They went absolutely nuts and jumped up to the 1st level, trying to pull us both over the railing. I swung my half empty champagne bottle into the side of a Nazi's head and he fell backwards onto the floor... surprisingly, the bottle didn't break. Someone yelled "FIGHT!" and dozens of Nazis started elbowing and kicking people in the Pit to reach us.

The crowd went nuts. Someone else yelled, "KILL THE NAZIS!" and suddenly everyone was swinging their champagne bottles. It was total chaotic mayhem. Someone grabbed my shoulder from behind and just before my fist connected with their face I realized it was one of the friends I'd come there with and pulled my punch.

"Oh my god, Queen! Someone just got stabbed in the Pit! We need to get out of here!" she yelled in my ear. We held onto each other, elbowing our way through the crowd to get outside. Somehow, we made it.

A couple of our friends were still inside, but as far as we were concerned those motherfuckers were on their own. Always stick with your group, and always have your friends' backs... thems the rules.

88

Aaron, the manager at *Fascinations* who handled my interview, began flirting with me. I felt a strong connection... strong enough that I broke my rule about never dating coworkers, although we both needed to keep our relationship secret. He was very cheerful and upbeat, a nice change from the mopey depressed motherfuckers I always hung out with. He was the first guy ever to take me out on an actual dinner dates to fancy restaurants. He treated me with respect, like a Lady.

When Courtney found out I was dating a guy she flipped out. She started fights with me constantly, arguing about the stupidest bullshit, often about nothing at all. After a few weeks of that I told her I was moving out. She calmed down a bit, stopped being such a psycho bitch, and things went back to normal for a little while. She seemed to be okay with it.

That weekend, Aaron drove his little Geo Tracker to our place to help me move. Courtney decided to make herself scarce. I walked outside, carrying a box, and said, "What's wrong with your tire?" Taking a closer look, we saw that all four tires were flat, with wide gashes stabbed through each sidewall. The psycho bitch had taken a kitchen knife to them!

"COURTNEY! Get your ass out here! I know you did this!" I yelled. The bushes across the street rustled. "You better get the fuck over here right fucking now!" I yelled. I saw her fat face pop out of the bushes, then she slowly waddled her little round Humpty Dumpty lookin' ass over to me, looking at me the way she did with those ignorant empty cow eyes. Something else took over... something that wanted to kill her.

My hand shot out and I grabbed her by the throat... no, not by the neck, but by her fucking trachea. I felt my fingers touch behind her windpipe and lifted her off the ground with one arm... I have no idea how I managed that, as she outweighed me, but she felt as light as a feather. She ineffectively tried swatting and kicking to free herself, but her stubby little arms and legs weren't long enough to reach. Her mouth gasped like a fish out of water, her eyelids fluttered, and she pissed herself as she lost consciousness. Suddenly, Aaron was next to me, wide eyed and pale as a ghost. "Carol! JAIL!" he yelled.

That woke me up. I blinked, then realized how fucking heavy she was. I opened my hand and she dropped to the sidewalk, moments before the first Denver police car rolled up, lights flashing. How the hell did they get here so fast?

It turned out my upstairs neighbor had called the cops 15 minutes earlier when she saw Courtney stabbing a butcher knife through Aaron's tires. Soon, she regained consciousness, saw the cops, and pretended to have a seizure. She was not epileptic and it was quite obvious to everyone she was faking... then she started yelling at the cops, going off on some bizarre unintelligible rant. They put the cuffs on her and took her in for a 72 hour psych hold.

Aaron needed to call *AAA* to tow his Tracker to a garage to have four tires mounted and balanced, but we had the next three days free to pack my stuff into his vehicle without further interruptions.

Aaron lived in an apartment complex in Saudi Aurora, near Illif and Chambers. Immediately after I moved in, he dreamed of a man in black with long black hair and eyes like burning flames standing in a hallway downstairs from him. He outstretched his hand and Aaron could feel his soul detach from his body and begin floating towards him. Aaron fought it and was able to snap back to his body, whereupon he woke up.

After recounting his dream to me, I stated, "That sounds like Azazel," and began telling him my backstory. He nodded, smiling politely, before proceeding to tell me that it seemed like a very intricate fantasy created by my subconscious mind, whereupon he proclaimed himself an agnostic and a skeptic who believed in the scientific method and demanded "proof." In other words, he felt it was all delusional bullshit. Great.

The Courtney fiasco was still fresh in our minds, Drake and his creepy friends continued to low key stalk me, and we both were dissatisfied with our jobs so we decided we needed a major life change.

We decided to move to Florida.

We moved into a trailer with a screened in porch in Chipley, Florida. It was a fairly nice trailer, surrounded by a pine forest. The back of the trailer was covered with spiderwebs, with hundreds of webs in the trees... needless to say, we never went in the backyard.

They were giant yellow Banana Spiders bigger than a tarantula. They rarely came inside, but when they did we could hear their feet running across the tile floor and feel their weight when they jumped on the bed... it was awful.

We both got jobs as "counselors" at a youth correctional facility for girls who had been adjudicated mentally ill, but many of them were perfectly sane. Apparently, if you try to kill your abusive stepfather for raping you that automatically means you're "crazy" in Florida.

The girls loved us because we would actually sit down and listen to them, treating them with respect, whereas the inbred locals would just beat them up and impose humiliating punishments like taking away their "privilege" to use soap and shampoo for a week. These ignorant Christian rednecks would perform "prescribed takedowns" on a daily basis, often several times daily. They refused to listen to anything they had to say. Whenever a girl had a complaint they would reply in a flat robotic voice, "You need to stop your activity right now," before twisting their arm behind their head and slamming them to the floor.

The only legitimate reason for performing a takedown is to break up a fight or to prevent a girl from harming herself or others. The staff would automatically do it anytime a girl "acted out" by raising her voice or crying, which was often... and understandable, considering their circumstances. During the entire year we worked here, I only performed two takedowns.

Many years later, long after they were released, a few of these girls still remembered me and looked me up on *Facebook*. They are on my "friends" list to this day.

91

Eventually, a *Hot Topic* opened up in the only shopping mall in nearby Panama City, so I dropped off my resume and due to my past experience and glowing references was immediately hired as a full time assistant manager. Within a few years I was running that store.

I went to six Gatherings while I was in Florida, travelling to campgrounds in Ohio and Illinois where we had a lot more freedom and privacy than in some fucking convention center surrounded by angry cops.

Each Gathering was a story in itself... unfortunately my memories of them are somewhat limited due to the fact that I was shitfaced drunk on *Black Magic* rum the whole time.

I was adopted by the notorious Cleveland Crew, who were like the OG Godfathers of the Juggalo Nation, after meeting a few of them at a truckstop. I thought they were just super cool guys, but noticed that no-one ever disrespected them or messed with them in any way. I later heard rumors they supposedly ran the infamous "Drug Bridge" at Cave of the Rock... but I never really saw any of that shit. They were my best friends and I always set up my tent at their site. They never called me Queen... they called me "THE QUEEN!" After a few years, with multiple medallions hanging from my neck, Juggalo gangsta ink, and solid affiliation with the Cleveland Crew, soon I was unofficially declared "Queen of the Juggalos."

A lot of celebrities would show up to the Gatherings, and were always offered all the free drugs and pussy they could eat. On different years, I saw both Charlie Sheen and Ron Jeremy running around nekkid, tripping balls and having a great time. It was awesome. Unfortunately I missed the year that Tia Tequila disrespected everyone so the Juggalos literally flung their own shit at her onstage then tried to set her trailer on fire, but the stupid bitch deserved it.

"Backyard wrestling" was popular back then, and Juggalos were constantly holding unauthorized matches all over the campground, hitting each other with folding chairs and busting florescent tubes over each other's heads. Surprisingly, hardly anyone got seriously hurt in these matches, but every year at least one Juggalo died: a few drowned trying to swim in the river, others ODed or passed out in their tent and died of dehydration... because people are stupid and shit happens.

Another thing you'd often see were "juggalettes" walking around half nekkid, wearing bikinis, lingerie, bodywebs... and none of them had to worry about getting groped or molested. They knew they were safe because anyone who messed with them would get beat the fuck down by any and all Juggalos in the immediate vicinity. We policed our own and even held court to sentence anyone accused of wrongdoing. Usually it was just stupid silly bullshit and they would make a fun game of it, letting the crowd vote on what their punishment should be... typically they would be told to "spin the wheel" and they would need to do whatever dare it said, or for more serious infractions they would be locked in a cage next to the stage during the performance and fans would spray them with Faygo.

One year someone was breaking into campers and cars, stealing cameras, laptops, plane tickets, anything of value. This was unheard of. This had never happened at a Gathering before. Word quickly spread to all the main crews. Soon, someone spotted this guy sneaking around like a ninja carrying a dufflebag. He was discretely shadowed until he was spotted opening the trunk of a car and hiding cameras and computers inside... then he headed out again with the empty dufflebag.

They did not have court for this guy... he got "Juggalo Justice."
They beat him nearly to death, then dragged him half nekkid and
unconscious to the gate and called the paramedics to transport
him to the ER. After that, they pried open the trunk of his car
and gave everyone back their missing stuff. Then they busted out
all the glass, tore off the doors, and drove over what was left with a
monster truck someone had driven up there. This provided over
an hour of entertainment for everyone, as well as a lesson to all.

When Jessey turned 16 I thought it was time for him to go to his
first Gathering. "Don't worry, we'll keep an eye out for yer boy,
yo..." the Cleveland Crew assured me. A couple hours later I saw
him wandering around in a daze, so high he didn't even recognize
me at first, but at least he was smiling.

"Are you doing alright, son?" I asked.

"Yeeeeeeah... I had a couple puffs off a fat doobie they called a
Jeffery... I am fucked the hell up, yo!"

"Jesus fuck..." A *Jeffery* was a giant rolling paper filled with a mix
of everything they were selling at the Drug Bridge, chopped up
and mixed with weed: acid, ecstasy, heroin, meth, angel dust,
probably even motherfucking bath salts for all anyone knew.

I made sure he stayed hydrated and didn't take anymore free
drugs for the rest of the night. He had a great time.

The Gathering was ALWAYS a great time.

92

A side project of *ICP* with *Twiztid* and several other bands called *Psychopathic Rydas* would perform wearing flannel shirts and covered with bandannas... the colors didn't matter, it was a faux gangsta rap project that sampled a lot of well known hip hop tracks... with permission of the original artists, many of whom performed at Gathering.

Anyway, they'd just released a new album and gave an amazing live performance that year. Their biggest hit was a song they called "Duk Da Fuk Down" in reference to doing drivebys with an Uzi submachinegun. For the rest of that Gathering, instead of greeting one another with the standard "Whoop whoop!" the Juggalos would yell "DUK DA FUK DOWN!" then laugh maniacally. It was so awesome I decided I needed to have "Duk Da Fuk Down" tattooed across my chest in thick black Olde English calligraphy like a *chola*. None of the White people in Florida could read it. When they asked me what it said I just told them it was "my name in Latin" which seemed like a good answer.

While I was managing the Panama City *Hot Topic*, every Sunday morning a group of young black guys would come in. First they would stop at Foot Locker to buy new sneakers, then would walk into my store to buy color coordinated band T-shirts off the wall to match. On this day one of them decided to buy a Hatchetman shirt.

"I'm sorry, but I cannot sell you this shirt unless you actually listen to *ICP*. Tell me one line of lyrics from any one of their songs and I will sell it to you."

"What? Are you serious?"

"Dead serious. I will gladly sell you any shirt you want off of those other walls, but these two rows of *ICP* shirts over here I will not sell to anyone who does not listen to the music." I wrote down a list of several songs. "Here are a few good ones you might like. Go listen to these, come back next week, and I can sell you a Hatchetman." He looked down at the list.

"Fo reals?"

"Yup." He shook his head, picked a different shirt, made his purchase and walked out. All of them looked at me like I was crazy.

The next week they were back, all smiles. "I bought their album and listened to it. Some of the songs were kinda stupid, but I liked a couple of them." Then he proceeded to sing me some lyrics. I sold him the Hatchetman shirt.

The week after that I was wearing a low cut shirt when they came in. His eyes went wide. "Daaaaaamn! Dat be some gangsta shit right there! DUK DA FUK DOWN!" Apparently black people could read the tattoo just fine and knew exactly what it meant. I wrote down the name of that album by *Psychopathic Rydas* and he bought it and thought it was great.

The following Sunday morning, the food court was very quiet as I waited for my Starbucks iced mocha latte to be made. Only a few very old ladies were there, sitting at tables with their tea and crumpets or whatever 90 year old great grandmothers order from the food court. Suddenly I hear a familiar voice shout out, "QUEEN!!!" then all five yelled, "DUK DA FUK DOWN!!!" followed by laughter as he and his crew proceeded to walk across the Mall to my store. One of the old ladies snorted tea out her nose and I swear another one may've had a mini stroke... even the barrista looked like he peed himself a little.

From that day forward, that was how they greeted me EVERY time they saw me. All five of them yelling like they were about to shoot up the Mall. It made my motherfucking day.

93

One afternoon I was at work in the back room, and kicked open the door to the store while holding two heavy boxes in one arm and a 6 foot aluminum ladder in the other, walking across the sales floor to hang new band shirts on the wall. As I unfolded the ladder a customer approached. He was a big guy with big muscles like a bodybuilder.

"Hi... ummmm... I'm sorry if this sounds out of line in any way, but have you ever thought about wrestling?"

"What?"

"I'm a semi-pro wrestler and I'd like to invite you to my show this weekend. I'd like you to consider being my manager. I need a strong woman who looks badassed like you." He gave me his card and wrote the address of the venue as well as a time and date on the back, then proceeded to buy a few hundred dollars worth of clothing items for his costume. He told me he was a firefighter and always played the part of the good guy, who in wrestling lingo was called the "face" while the bad guy was the "heel." Half of the act was scripted and it was always predetermined who would win, but often the unexpected would happen and sometimes they would actually fight for real... there really wasn't much oversight.

Anyway, I showed up at the place expecting to watch a free show, and somehow was convinced to step into the ring to act as his manager... which basically meant I was supposed to announce him and whip up the audience, getting them excited, making them cheer.

The script said that he was supposed to lose this match, and the heel played the bad guy, pulling a bunch of dirty tricks and doing a few illegal moves. My guy pretended to be knocked out and needed to be dragged from the ring by his friends. The heel mocked him and began hamming it up, smiling to a chorus of outraged BOOOOOOOs. Then he strutted down the aisle to the dressing room.

Something snapped inside my head. I vaulted over the ropes and chased that motherfucker down. He turned, a look of horrified shock on his face... this wasn't in the script! He didn't even know who the fuck I was. I leaped on him, wrapping my legs around his chest and slamming my elbow down on top of his head, but pulling my punch at the last second... he stumbled and we both fell through the door.

The crowd went absolutely nuts.

I became an immediate addition to the act and began attending practice sessions several times a week. I wrestled men in a few matches under the name "Uzzi." Everyone thought I named myself after the submachinegun, and I never corrected them. Floridans are creepy weird with their religion and I didn't feel comfortable going there yet.

My signature finishing move was the "Donkey Punch Monkey Flip" which is sort of like a piledriver. First, I'd fling my opponent into the corner turnbuckle... then I'd charge across the ring and jump, planting my feet on top of his thighs while I faked a brutal hammerfist to the top of his head... and he faked being dazed from a concussion. Then, I'd grab him behind his neck with both hands, roll backwards as we hit the mat, then LAUNCH that motherfucker with my feet. I had incredibly powerful legs and they would literally end up flying out of the ring, usually under the ropes, sometimes over them. It was a lot of fun.

After a few months I had assembled my own team, most of whom were crazy Juggalos. We all wore facepaint and called ourselves "The Freakshow" and I became "Uzzi the Ringmaster" and wore a white pimp suit and carried a pimp stick. I did not wrestle as much in matches anymore, but we still beat the hell out of each other in practice and I played the "mean manager" who would beat up her own guys when they lost. The audience alternatively loved and hated us depending on how the script ran, sometimes we were the good guys, sometimes we were the heels.

One night, we decided to do something completely different. A new wrestler had just joined The Freakshow, but in order to make it official we needed to "initiate" him in front of a live audience on stage. Nobody in the audience had any idea what we were doing and we hadn't shown the script to anyone, so there was a lot of shocked confusion when this guy fell to his knees, opened a *King James Bible*, and swore an oath to "sell his soul" to Uzzi the Ringmaster, whereupon a hidden pyrotechnic charge was detonated and the Bible burst into flames! The deeply religious audience did not think it was nearly as awesome as we did and we were BOOOOOOed throughout the rest of our act. I didn't care. Fuck those unappreciative dipshits... this was showbiz!

94

Panama City began to bore me. Every day at work was the same, the wrestling wasn't as fun anymore, and after coming home from his job at *Game Stop*, Aaron would just want to play videogames and watch DVDs and never do anything else or go anywhere. I was bored and dissatisfied with the dead end rut my life was stuck in.

I took out a student loan to go to trucker school for 6 weeks so I could get my CDL, then was hired on at *Werner* pending completion of an additional 6 weeks training, but first there was a week of Orientation... most of which simply involved waiting around in a hotel room with another new hire.

Jesus fuck, you would not believe the mutants they hired. The first person they paired me with was an angry crazy fat lady who chainsmoked 5 packs of generic cigarettes a day and never used the ashtray, flinging butts everywhere, including into my bed and luggage. Then she had the audacity to try ordering me around. I told *Werner* to find me another room or I would sleep in the hallway, so next they paired me with this homeless anorexic woman whose luggage was a trash bag and who had duct tape wrapped around her feet instead of shoes. How they made it through the hiring process I do not know, but apparently they each had a CDL and a heartbeat.

"Training" meant going on the road as a team driver with a trainer. I was terrified. We had heard all sorts of horror stories during Orientation about how there were no female trainers so you needed to be paired with some guy, and sometimes they would refuse to stop for bathroom breaks or showers and occasionally trainees were beaten up or raped. Just that week a *Werner* trainer was in the news for having chained his trainee in the sleeper behind the curtains with **BDSM** restraints and basically kidnapped, tortured, and raped her the whole 6 weeks, apparently making her wear adult diapers and wiping her down with baby wipes or something.

My assigned trainer was Tom, the same name as my brother, which I thought was a good omen. He was a huge guy, about 6'5" 350# and older. Fortunately he was super nice and really cool. He introduced himself as a retired cop and said, "You never need to worry about me, and if I ever do or say anything that makes you feel uncomfortable please let me know." He was true to his word, a good and honorable man.

He taught me a lot of old skool trucker tricks that no-one knows anymore: the CB lingo, the various flashing light codes, how to improvise repairs on the road, and how to react in adverse conditions. Things like the many uses of WD40, spraying the tires with bleach when the roads were too slick, jake brake settings, chaining tires, and how to feather and tap the trolley brake to pull yourself out of a jackknife. The new breed of drivers doesn't even know what half the switches and levers on their dashboards do, and most cannot even shift a manual transmission so many companies have switched to automatics.

Tom's truck was a land yacht... a Freightliner Classic XL, the biggest truck on the road at that time, because, "I'm a big guy so I need a big truck!" It had 13 gears and was twice the size of an International. That is what I learned to drive on, and I learned a lot.

One of the scariest situations I'd ever found myself in happened late at night on Cabbage Mountain around the notorious "Deadman's Pass." No chain law was in effect yet, and I hit some black ice and the trailer jackknifed and, without even thinking about it, I tapped the trolley brake lever to lock the rear wheels on the trailer which straightened us out and kept us from flying over a 500 foot cliff. As soon as my heart started beating again, I pulled over, got out, and proceeded to smoke 3 cigarettes in 3 minutes before getting back in the truck. I was shaking so badly I couldn't continue, so I woke Tom up. "Are we there already?" he asked.

"We almost died. I can't do this. You need to drive." I said.

"Well, thanks for not killing us. You did everything perfectly. I will drive us the rest of the way this time, but you just proved you got what it takes to do this."

The next time we almost died was coming down the mountain from Leadville. The DOT road report said to expect "patches of snow" and again, no chain law in effect. Bullshit. We ran into almost a hundred miles of unplowed roads, over ice, with multiple hairpin turns. Once, the trailer nearly spun off the road and pulled us over the edge... if our tandems hadn't been all the way forward we would've dropped a thousand feet. Moving the tandems brought our back wheels forward by ten feet, and they just barely cleared the edge... the ass end of the trailer swung out over the abyss and we lived. We needed to adjust them due to load weight and California law... if our destination was in another state or we had been given a lighter load the wheels would've been back in their normal position and my story would've ended right there.

Honestly, most of the time driving truck is pretty boring, just driving along endless highways, getting stuck in traffic jams, and waiting for hours to be loaded or unloaded, but sometimes you almost die, and on rare occasions something truly amazing happens.

The best experience I have ever had, or ever will have, as a trucker was as a rookie driver in New York City. NYC is a maze of one way streets, low overpasses, and streets where trucks are absolutely forbidden to go. Add to that equation confusing street signs, random construction detours, and psychotic motorists. In short, NYC is a fucking nightmare to maneuver a big truck through and many drivers flat out refuse to deliver there.

Anyway, there I am, with absolutely no idea where the fuck I'm going, and Tom tells me I need to make a right turn... but there was a little Jaguar XJ-S convertible in a No Parking red zone right at the corner and I couldn't clear it. No amount of maneuvering could get us around that stupid little sports car. I applied the air brakes, put on my hazard lights, and waited. Traffic came to a halt.

Soon, a very pissed off Italian NYPD traffic cop ran up and began yelling at me. "Whadda yoo dooin? Move dis fookin truck outta da way!"

"But... there's a car parked in my way... and I can't back up or go forward... I'm stuck." He looked at the Jaguar, got even angrier than before, then yelled, "CAH? I DON'T SEE NO FOOKIN' CAH! YOU MOVE DIS TRUCK RIGHT NOW!" My jaw dropped. I turned to look at Tom. He was laughing his ass off.

"This is New Yawk City... the cops give zero fucks here... go for it, Crusher." I was able to turn the cab around the corner fine, but the whole truck rocked and shook as the two duallies at the back of the trailer rolled over the top of that Yuppiemobile, completely destroying it. As we continued down the road I looked in the mirror and saw the cop scribbling out a ticket and sticking between the remains of the wiper blade and windshield... then he scribbled out a second ticket and started on a third. I busted out laughing. It was one of the best moments of my life.

95

After training was over, I parted ways with Tom and was assigned a 379 longnosed Peterbuilt. It was purple and had 13 gears. I absolutely loved that truck and had a giant chrome Hatchetman put on the grille. I drove it to the Gathering and everyone went nuts over it.

What I did not love was the fact that the pay was absolute shit. I never got the miles I needed and was falling behind on my bills. I began putting out applications elsewhere.

Eventually, another *Werner* driver who I had met a few times at terminals and spoke to occasionally on the phone was given an offer of better pay at *J.B. Hunt* as a team driver and asked if I was interested in going over the road with him. After clarifying that our relationship would remain strictly professional, I agreed.

Holy fucking shit, what a nightmare that turned out to be. This fucker couldn't drive for shit, couldn't read a map, and had no idea how the trailers needed to be loaded... plus he was tweaked out of his mind on meth. Whenever we took a break at a truckstop he would wander off, then come back wired off his ass to proceed driving 70 mph down winding mountain roads on the other side of the double yellow line while I was trying to sleep in the back... and then he would get lost.

I knew I was in serious trouble when we picked up a paper load and he handled everything while I was sleeping. These giant rolls of paper weigh 7,000 pounds each and there were six of them in the back... and a new hire had loaded our trailer so they were not loaded ends facing up like rolls are supposed to be... they were all laying on their sides! He had attached a pair of ratchet straps to the final roll and put down a block of wood to prevent 42,000# of giant paper rolls laying on their sides from bashing through the flimsy back doors and killing everyone behind us after the first sharp turn we took. "It is fine," he said. No... it most fucking certainly was NOT fine! And, in order to guarantee the back of our trailer was blasted open by runaway paper rolls, he had routed us through the mountains... during a blizzard.

I made him pull over and we called dispatch, who told us to run it. I said no fucking way, at the very least we need to re-route, which they reluctantly approved. Amazingly, we made it all the way to the delivery point without incident.

He was fucking up constantly, swerving all over the road at insanely high speeds, I am amazed he never wrecked. Then I would wake up to find him on some "NO TRUCKS" road in Los Angeles where they would ding you with a ten thousand dollar fine. The final straw came at a truckstop in St Louis. I was suffering from heavy sleep deprivation because I kept being slammed around inside the sleeper whenever we took a curve. We were parked at a *Flying J* for the night and I was trying to sleep, but this incessant tap tap tapping kept coming from the driver seat, where he was typing on his laptop keyboard with one hand while tapping a pen against the steering wheel with the other. "Could you PLEASE not do that? I really need my sleep."

"I can use my laptop if I want." I blew my motherfucking top, ripping that mask clean off to show him what was beneath.

"YOU ARE DRIVING ME TO FLORIDA RIGHT FUCKING NOW, MOTHERFUCKER, OR I AM GOING TO STAB YOU IN THE FUCKING THROAT, TOSS YOU IN THE BUSHES, AND TELL EVERYONE YOU NEVER CAME BACK AFTER GOING OFF WITH ONE OF THOSE LOT LIZARDS YOU BUY DRUGS FROM!!!" He went absolutely white... then he looked down and saw the knife in my hand.

We were not authorized to be driving and were scheduled to pick up a load the next day, but this was before ELDs and we were on paper logs. He drove me all the way to Panama City, apologizing the whole way and thanking me for not killing him after he dropped me off outside town with my stuff. I called Aaron to pick me up, then I called *J.B. Hunt* to tell them I quit. This trucking thing just didn't work out.

96

I returned to *Hot Topic* as an assistant manager, as that was the best opportunity available to me in Panama City at that time. Aaron continued his job as a manager at *Game Stop*, then would return home to play videogames all day. The drudgery was draining my will to live.

A few of the girls I worked with were on a roller derby team and invited me to join them. It sounded like fun, so I said what the hell. It was awesome.

Because I am so big and angry, they made me a "blocker" and I excelled in that capacity, knocking bitches out the way. Then both teams would meet at a pub afterwards and celebrate together like we were all best friends. It was wonderful.

Unfortunately, nothing good ever lasts. 4 months later I fell during a training session and hurt myself bad... so bad I couldn't walk. I fractured my pelvis. "Omigod! Queen! We need to get you to the hospital!" they cried.

"Fuck that... I ain't got no insurance and they can't do anything for a cracked pelvis except bill me thousands of dollars for Xrays and pills... just carry me outside and help me into my car." I couldn't move my right leg without using both hands to press it down on the gas... eventually, I managed to get it shifted into 2nd gear and I stayed in 2nd all the way home, then leaned on the horn until Aaron came outside to help me.

I needed to take a week off from work to lay in bed and eat Motrin, but at least I got a week's vacation pay for it, although I'd had other plans. I went back to work, hobbling around on a cane for a while. Eventually I gained my strength back.

My friends told me they really needed a Head Referee and thought I would be perfect... it did not require much skating, other players were forbidden from hitting you, and refs did not need to participate in practice sessions. I felt I was well enough to do this, so I was the Head Referee for three years and our team won games at the State Championship every year, but never took the title. I was just happy to be getting out of the house. It was not nearly as fun as knocking bitches out the way, but it was a far more important job. I was proud of being Head Referee.

One night, after a derby match, we were at the pub and I saw a man sitting at the bar with sigils tattooed on his neck and arms. He said he was from out of town and just passing through. He was super intense. We had an interesting conversation about spiritual matters and I showed him the seals tattooed on the back of my leg.

He fixed me with his gaze and stated, "There's nothing here but stagnation. This is a dead zone. I'm not staying and neither should you." Then he got up and left without another word.

I got the strong impression he had been sent specifically to find me and pass along that message.

98

I met Anubis at *Hot Topic*. He came in to buy shirts occasionally, and we began talking. Eventually the topics shifted to spiritual matters. He had a strong interest in several areas with a solid connection to the Egyptian god of Death.

It was refreshing to be able to have conversations like this after almost a decade of being condescendingly told by Aaron that it "was all in my head."

After many discussions, several readings, and a regression, we determined that Anubis had been destined to find me and serve as my protector. I did not understand exactly why that was, but our connection was solid and my readings have always been accurate.

I told him I was planning on returning to Denver and he expressed an interest in moving there as well. "The energy there is crazy, like nothing you've ever seen. Expect heavy shit to start popping off as soon as you get there. Every time I swung through on a hometime it was nuts." He said he understood and was ready to face whatever.

He had no idea.

Jessey had just graduated high school and announced he wanted to go trainhopping. Most people vaguely understand that hopping freights or "riding the rails" is a dangerous pastime, but you have no idea.

First of all, people frequently die doing this. A lot of people fall onto the track and have the metal wheels run over them, cutting them in half or severing a limb. People are beaten, robbed, raped, and murdered by hobos all the time... there was even a murderous hobo gang called "Freight Train Riders of America" with over a thousand members who rode the rails from coast to coast. You can be beaten and arrested by Railroad Police, who are basically private security guards with a license to kill and plenty of places to dispose of the bodies. There were even serial killers riding the rails, one of which, "Sidetrack," was active at that time. And on top of all that you never knew exactly where the trains were heading, what climate you were heading into, if you might be locked inside a car, or if the car might just be parked in a trainyard for weeks in the heat or cold. There were a thousand ways to die out there.

I never trainhopped, but I had many friends who did, and they told me about various tricks they used to stay alive. I told Jessey that he was an adult now since he had just turned 18, so I could not stop him, but as his mother I needed to teach him a few things first to help him stay safe, which I did.

I gave him a lockblade, my acoustic guitar which he had been learning to play, and a cheap flip phone, then gave him some water bottles and granola bars to put in his pack. When he left I was unsure if I'd ever see my son again.

100

The distance between myself and Aaron widened to a chasm. While he stated he "respected my beliefs" and never openly mocked them, he continued to speak to me in a condescending manner, implying that my spiritual experiences were mere delusions. I could never discuss this part of my life without being made to feel as if I was mentally ill.

His family was far worse. They were very well to do and proper, with smug superior attitudes, and being respectable Christians absolutely hated the fact that I was pagan. Every time I went to a family event, they would waste no time in surrounding me, peppering me with snide intrusive questions about my beliefs, my tattoos, my piercings, demanding to know what everything "meant" as if they were accumulating evidence and passing judgment. It always felt like an interrogation. Sometimes, I would overhear his mother saying things to Aaron like, "Why are you still with her?"

This had been ongoing from the day they met me and continued for the entire decade we were in Florida. They openly hated me, without any cause other than the fact that I looked different and was not of their religion. Myself and Aaron struggled on our meager paychecks and whenever there was a crisis we needed to rely on friends, take out a predatory Payday Loan, or have a bill sent to collections because his wealthy family would not give us a dime. They seemed to think of it as "Tough Love" in order to make him see the error of his ways. Regardless, to his credit Aaron was loyal and steadfast and refused to leave me.

I liked Aaron, he had a good heart, but he was complacent and lacked any motivation to better himself or set any goals, he didn't even want to leave the house on his days off. He was perfectly content to remain in his comfortable rut at his dead end job, immersing himself in games and movies rather than actually going out and experiencing life.

I made up my mind to leave him. We were holding each other back. If I left, he could find another girl who was more like him, a girl who would marry him and give him children which would overjoy his hateful parents and compel them to shower him with riches. I just needed to get the fuck out of Florida. I felt like I was drowning. Literally. The last place we lived had a black mold infestation, which infected my lungs and made it difficult to breathe whenever it was humid, which was often.

Florida was killing me.

I took a second job driving a taxi to save up enough money to move back to Denver.

101

Driving taxi was hard and dirty... but I made bank, and soon quit *Hot Topic* altogether. We didn't rent the cab, we were expected to split the fares with the company and pay for our own gas, but could keep all our tips. They did not do much business in Panama City, but I got hired shortly before Spring Break and was packing 8 or 9 drunk college kids in my cab at once. I felt like a dirty old man, slowly rolling down the street with my windows down, shouting out to people "Where you wanna go? I'll take you all for two bucks each."

Sometimes drunks would puke in the cab and refuse to pay the hundred dollar cleanup fee, so I would drive them outside of town and park on a bridge and tell them, "The cops are on the way, you can get arrested for failure to pay and public intoxication, or you can pay me a hundred bucks." It pissed me off because there was always a wastebasket in the back and they never used it. Once they paid, I would let them out and drive off... and it was a long walk back to town in the dark, but fuck them. A hundred bucks didn't even cover the fares and tips I lost in an hour, let alone the bullshit of cleaning up their chuck and deodorizing the cab.

Eventually, I was assigned a minivan with dark tinted windows and could fit 25 college kids in that motherfucker. They were all like, "But we can't all fit in there!"

"Trust me, I can make this work... you all wanna get to the PARTY, right?"

"YEAH!" I would tell everyone exactly where to sit. I had drunk sorority girls in the cargo compartment and sitting on the laps of girls who were sitting on other people's laps. The cargo van would hold twenty five passengers... unless they were fat. I learned that by playing the right station and singing along with them I could get much better tips. Afterwards, my boss would sometimes ask me how many passengers were in the van that trip.

"Six... I had six passengers."

Things got crazy during Spring Break. There was fierce competition between transportation services as everyone made all their money during those months, then lived on poverty wages the rest of the year. Often another taxi would pull up and offer to take them for a few dollars less, and we were authorized to haggle in situations like that not so as to lose the fare entirely. I heard stories that some cabbies got very aggressive and actually were opening doors and trying to take passengers out of other cabs into theirs, but that never happened to me. I would've shanked any motherfucker who tried that shit with me.

I made more money during those three months than I had ever made in my life. After a good shift, I would go home, throw a thousand dollars in small bills all over my bed, then strip nekkid and roll around in it. I was straight ballin, yo, like a motherfuckin PIMP.

I got a call from Jessey one day. He told me he had run into a few issues getting trespass citations for being caught on freight cars in train yards, but nothing especially horrible had transpired. Currently, he was in Oregon, and super excited to tell me about a music festival he'd attended that weekend.

"MOMS! I was at the festival and this cool dude asked if I wanted a puff off his joint, and I was like, DUDE! You're Juicy J from *THREE 6 MAFIA!* And he was like, How you know who I is? And I say my MOMS listens to you. Is she black? Naw, but her dad is black and she grew up in the hood. Dat cool, he said. MOM! I SMOKED A JOINT WITH JUICY J!"

"That's awesome, son. I'm glad to hear you're having a great time."

"Oh, it gets even better! Mom, I met this MIDGET! And she was like, You wanna smoke a joint with me? And I said okay... then she was like, Do you wanna walk me to my campsite and see my 1970s custom Shag Van? And I was like, okay. MOM! I MET A MIDGET AND SHAGGED HER IN HER SHAG VAN!!!" I was speechless for a few moments, taken aback by the enormity of this accomplishment.

"Outstanding... your world is now complete." He babbled on a while longer, still riding the wave. He promised to call again in a few weeks and we said our goodbyes.

My son smoked a joint with Juicy J and shagged a midget in her Shag Van on the same weekend. I cannot lie... there were tears in my eyes. That was the proudest moment of my life.

103

Soon, it was time to bid farewell to Aaron and Panama City. I had managed to save about $20,000 cash, enough to rent a moving truck and put down a deposit on a Denver apartment.

I had a job waiting for me there, driving a van for *Super Shuttle,* a taxi service who exclusively ran vans between Downtown and DIA. My brother worked for them, and his friend leased a van and drove 12 hours a day and said I could drive the other 12 if I wanted. It was practically guaranteed, I just needed to fill out some paperwork and get the necessary endorsement and permits.

Aaron was sullen and resentful, he hated change and did not understand why we needed to part ways. I told him his family would never accept me and he needed to find a nice girl who was more acceptable to them and matched his sedentary unambitious lifestyle... although I phrased it a bit differently than that.

He was like a fully grown child, whining, pleading, clinging, sucking the life out of me... but I felt badly about leaving him anyway. He had always treated me well and had not done anything wrong... but he really hadn't done much of anything at all. Every day was exactly the same. He had not grown, changed, evolved.

I was in Florida for ten years. It is true that it was a spiritual dead zone, no portals or significant activity at all, even though I continued to perform rituals and had dozens of sigils and seals tattooed into my flesh during my time here. It gave me a break, a respite, a safe place to recover, heal, and grow. I learned a lot free from constant spiritual interference and invasion. Aaron provided security and stability while allowing me the freedom to wrestle, skate, and get my CDL. Thank you Aaron.

He continued to call me on the phone for years and we were friends on *Facebook* until he married a beautiful young lady who was everything I wasn't, and his family began lavishing them with extravagant gifts: a house, new cars, vacations overseas. He completely ignored my comments and posts now. I thought it best that I stop following his page and defriended him. It hurt to see how much his family actually hated me. I sincerely wish him the best in his new life.

104

I arrived in Denver and immediately secured a small one bedroom apartment in a complex at Leetsdale and Quebec for $800 a month, then went down to *Super Shuttle* headquarters to submit my paperwork.

It was all a game to them... the "Let's make Queen run around in circles while pissing on her and telling her it's raining" game. For MONTHS they jerked me around... always more forms to fill out, tests, permits, certifications, background checks, physicals, all of which I was expected to pay for without reimbursement. Then they would never reply to messages or call me back. I would keep needing to go back to headquarters to follow up on my application, and they would be like "You just need one more thing before we can hire you," and after I'd submit it I'd hear nothing for weeks, then I'd go back and it would be, "Just one more thing."

I did not have a car and was taking cabs and the bus everywhere, so this was not only extremely inconvenient but was seriously pissing me off. It soon became abundantly clear that they had absolutely no intention of ever hiring me. It had been four months, my savings was nearly depleted, and in my despair I had been drinking myself to death, consuming a full bottle of *Black Magic* rum every night.

I could not continue like this. We were in the midst of an economic Recession and the only other jobs available were part-time and minimum wage. I resigned myself to going back on the road. I submitted my resume to *Knight Transportation* and was driving truck coast to coast once again.

I was basically paying $800 a month for a storage unit with a shower. None of my boxes from Florida had been unpacked and my only furniture was a dresser and my German buffet altar... I had been sleeping on an air mattress on the floor.

At that time, *Knight* was a far better company than *Werner* or *J B Hunt* and I was making good money, over a thousand dollars a week on average. I would return to Denver once every six or seven weeks and throw money around at the clubs like Pimp Sugah Momma, buying everyone drinks and treating people to breakfast at the diner afterwards, but before that I would always get my hair and nails did and buy several new outfits. I'd show up with three grand in my wallet and blow it all in four days. I became very popular. I'd show up at the club and everyone would yell "QUEEN!" and I would have a circle of hangers on who would always be demanding my time, my counsel, and favors like small loans to be repaid never.

I didn't care. It was good to be back in Denver. It was good to be the Queen.

105

I drove for *Knight* for two years. I would meet other *Knight* drivers at the terminals and made a few friends whom I exchanged numbers with and sometimes we would call one another on the road when we were bored. Driving is frequently boring, sitting in that seat 10-12 hours every day, sometimes struggling to stay awake, desperate for any distraction. It was important to have people you could call to pass the time.

One such driver I met at the *Knight* terminal with his 11 year old boy in tow... he approached and stated he felt he "needed" to talk to me, but seemed nice, normal, safe. I began running into him frequently as we seemed to deliver to the same places on the same days... it was uncanny how often we began running into one another. He told me he felt that we "knew each other in a past life," but I did not get that impression at all.

One day I delivered at a factory in rural Louisiana and he was also there. I was out of hours, with an empty trailer and no load scheduled for pickup, so I was stuck for a minimum of 10 hours and there was absolutely nothing around, no truckstop, no convenience store, just a dirt lot with an outhouse. He told me that if I wanted to park at another vacant lot ten miles away, his ex wife could pick us up and take us to her house where we could have a cookout and I could shower and sleep on the couch before being driven back in the morning. That sounded like a great option so I agreed.

She picked us up in her car shortly thereafter and drove us to the house, which was only about a mile away. The house was nice, but appeared strangely empty as if it was unlived in and being presented by a Realtor to potential buyers, but their children were there and everything seemed safe and normal. I was able to take a private shower and change into clean clothes for the first time in a week, which was appreciated.

We grilled steaks and burgers on the grill and each had a glass of red wine while engaged in light generic conversation, mostly about the trucking industry. Since I would not be driving until the next day I had two glasses. Out of the blue, he suddenly made an off topic comment I found very odd, "I just want people to know that I am a benevolent being." Then the conversation resumed in a normal direction and it was soon forgotten.

After dinner, he handed me a fresh glass of wine and the conversation continued for a while, then his ex-wife got up, said her goodbyes, and walked out the door with the kids and drove off. I did not expect her to leave, I had thought she lived there, but apparently that was no longer the case. I was uncomfortable being alone with this man I barely knew, and I was ever so dizzy... everything was foggy... like moving through a dream. It wasn't the wine... I barely felt the first two half glasses and had only taken a few sips from the third... I had difficulty moving my limbs, talking, or even remaining conscious. I got up, staggered over to the couch, and collapsed.

I sat on the couch, fading in and out of consciousness, as he sat across from me, staring at me with big wide eyes... but he didn't look scared or concerned... he looked hungry. I got the impression of a coiled snake about to strike. He began asking me questions, not about how I felt or if I was okay, but prying, probing questions of a spiritual nature, as if it were an interrogation. My limbs felt like lead, heavy and unresponsive, and when I tried to speak my words were slurred and garbled.

Ever see those Asian horror movies about ghosts, like *Ringu* and similar? You know how the evil ghost would cross a room? They would be standing there, then it was like you blinked and suddenly they'd teleported a few feet closer without moving their legs, then *pop* they teleport another few feet. That was what this motherfucker did, likely due to the synapses of my brain misfiring due to whatever he'd dosed my drink with. This reptilian motherfucker, locking eyes with me, suddenly teleported from his seat to crouched on the floor... then he popped a few feet closer... then he was looming directly over me. It was just like watching a horror movie, but through my own eyes.

As he sat beside me, he caressed my face and spoke in a low flat monotone, as if he was attempting to induce a hypnotic trance. "It's good to release control sometimes, you're full of walls and you don't know why... it's good to release control." I could not move or talk, but the silver charm bracelet I was wearing had a protective talisman and a Labradorite bead, which I managed to clutch in my hand, knowing it was my only hope... I couldn't even form a coherent thought let alone scream for help or call a Brethren. He was staring directly into my eyes, there was no way he could've seen what I was doing, but without taking his eyes off mine, he seized my hand and roughly pried my fingers open, letting the talisman fall free. "Open the straight jacket and release control... it feels good."

He unbuttoned my dress and placed a hand on my breast. I tried to move, to struggle, and failed. "Shhhhh... let it go..." He climbed atop me, pinning my arms with his knees, kissing the side of my neck. My eyes went out of focus as they teared up, I tried screaming but couldn't make a sound. He tugged my panties down to the ankles, leaving them there to restrain me from kicking. "You want this, don't you..." He slipped a finger inside me, then made a big production of tasting it, telling me how wonderful it was and how much he missed it. I blacked out, then briefly regained consciousness while he was raping me. He kept repeating the same phrase over and over in a robotic monotone: *"I am benevolent... I am benevolent... I am benevolent..."* I blacked out again.

My next memory was of him picking me up, carrying me across the house, and placing me in a bathtub where he proceeded to run the water and scrub off every trace of his DNA. I lost consciousness in the tub.

Some time later, I awoke on the couch... he had put back on my dress and buttoned it up as if nothing had happened. Rohypnol and GHB often wipe a victim's memory, so perhaps he actually expected me to suspect nothing. I had a smashing headache. He was snoring away, sound asleep on the other couch.

I stood up, unsteady on my feet, unable to maintain my balance. I put on my Converse, expecting him to wake up at any moment and tackle me... I did not think he intended to let me leave and I was unarmed and too weak to fight. Quietly, I made my way to the kitchen and began opening drawers... all the knives were gone. He was still snoring and my brain was too fogged to think clearly. I wanted to kill him, but his ex wife knew my name and with my piercings and tattoos I would be easy to describe. I thought about calling the police, but I was in a strange city in the Deep South and he was a local. There was nothing for me to do but escape. Fortunately, I remembered which direction my truck was in and it wasn't very far.

I had my hours back, but was still stuck on layover without a load. I knew that as soon as he woke up he would immediately run to the lot... and the thing about the International trucks we used was that all the door keys were interchangeable, so he could get inside my locked truck. Between my dizziness and the throbbing headache I was in no condition to drive, but drive I did, all the way to the nearest major truckstop which was about 30 miles away.

Later that evening, he called me... I did not answer and he did not leave a voicemail. A couple nights later he tried calling again. I never told anyone. I never saw or heard from that driver again. I quit driving shortly afterwards.

106

Anubis had moved to Denver and rented an apartment, so I would always hang out with him on my hometimes. After the rape, I had a bit of a mental breakdown and knew I needed to come off the road but didn't want to return to *Hot Topic* a third time.

There was an amazing high end clothing store on the 16th Street Mall called *Fusion Federation* which sold designer outfits, corsets, hats, and expensive shoes. Every time I came into town I would putter around the store for hours, buy a few things, and ask the manager if they were hiring because I desperately wanted to work there.

Myself and Anubis had been discussing spiritual matters and the topic of my nemesis AZAZEL came up. Anubis recognized the name and told me he saw a movie about him a few years earlier, *Fallen*, in which he would take possession of a human and could instantly *jump* into another person's body simply by brushing a single finger against them. Throughout the film, he would whistle "Time is On My Side" by *The Rolling Stones*. I had seen that film as well, it was one of my favorites, and we talked about it for awhile.

A few days later, we were walking together, but several feet apart, along the 16th Street Mall when I heard the distinctive whirr of skateboard wheels closing in behind us. Without a word, we both took another step further apart and the skateboard zipped between us, the young man on it had both arms spread wide, fingers apart, nearly grazing us... then, as soon as he passed, guess what song he began whistling? *Time is On My Side.*

"Holy shit!" Anubis said. "Did that just happen?"

"I warned you about Denver," I reminded him.

We walked into my favorite shop, *Fusion Federation*, and once again I asked if they were hiring.

They were, and hired me on the spot.

I telephoned *Knight* immediately afterwards to tell them I'd be cleaning out my truck.

107

I could feel Azazel's presence several times a week riding the RTD bus home from work. I could feel eyes boring into the back of my head, but whenever I turned to look I never saw anyone who stood out as being fixated on me. Several times I noticed a young heavyset guy with a flatcap and gauged earlobes, but he was always absorbed in his phone, never looking directly at me. This was ongoing for two years and will be addressed in more detail later.

Sometimes he would send me clear reminders that he was always around. Azazel is a *jumper* which means that he can instantly take over almost anyone's body, but unlike that silly movie there is no need for him to directly touch one possessed body to another... that is some straight up comic book bullshit right there.

He can take over anyone, anytime, for a few minutes. There are strict rules against this sort of thing, making him a criminal amongst demonkind subject to sanctions and punishment, but there is little real oversight and he has never given a shit over that sort of thing... apparently he has accumulated a few "free passes" to stay out of trouble on the rare occasions it becomes an issue.

Anyway, drunks, substance abusers, and the mentally ill have no focus or free will in that state and are super easy to manipulate or even completely take over. It happens a lot, and the usual rules do not seem to apply to street bums because nobody really gives a shit about what happens to them. Azazel's minions would jump into bums a lot, both to keep tabs on me and to make threats or send messages.

Denver's 16th Street Mall is basically a wide pedestrian street which covers a dozen blocks with an RTD trolley running back and forth down the middle and shops along either side, sort of like the biggest strip mall in America... and it has always been completely infested with bums, hobos, street kids, drug addicts, and schizophrenics, many of whom are homeless, transients, or residents of one of the many local shelters or "assisted living" facilities. They all tended to gravitate to the 16th Street Mall, which was in close proximity to Civic Center Park and the "Hug a Bum" Public Library.

Interacting with bums is an everyday occurrence on the Mall, which is where I worked. Panhandlers would approach me at least a dozen times a day, and I usually just ignored them or told them no, but sometimes an old broken down hobo who was beyond all hope only wanted a cigarette... so I would give him one, because that's just what you do. However, my cigarettes are expensive so I made a rule limiting the cigarettes I gave out to no more than three a day. Certainly not giving anyone my last smoke!

These drunken bums were all fucked up. They had been living on the streets for decades, eating scraps from trash bins and drinking *Thunderbird* fortified wine, their livers destroyed, their unwashed flesh covered with warts and cancerous rot, their dull rheumy eyes clouded with mucus and cataracts. They were beyond all help and would die alone on the streets. I felt sorry for the old timers who never demanded handouts or became aggressive. They weren't hurting anyone and it is a crime against humanity that the government does not take better care of people like that. Some of them are in motherfucking wheelchairs.

Sometimes I would be giving one of the walking dead a cigarette and suddenly they would transform. Their entire posture would change as they stood straighter, the structure of their face would become sharper, and their cloudy eyes would suddenly clear and lock on me, alert, focused, intelligent, not like a mush brained hobo's at all, before Azazel's message would come through in a single clear articulate sentence:

"I'm watching you..."

"I'm coming for you..."

"The time is near..."

Then their eyes would cloud over once again, their face would soften, their shoulders would hunch, and they would shuffle off, oblivious to what had just transpired.

This happened on a near weekly basis, several times while Anubis or others were with me as witnesses. He never wanted me to forget that he considered me his. It kept me on edge, suspicious of everyone. I always expected one of these crazy hobos to pull out a kitchen knife and attack me, but fortunately that never happened. The only reason it didn't was because Azazel wanted me alive. The worst thing about this was *I couldn't tell anyone...* no-one would ever believe me... only "crazies" thought things like this was real.

Eventually, circumstances of the everchanging Denver housing market had both myself and Anubis looking for a new place. We decided to pool our resources and move into a small apartment on 11th Avenue near Quebec.

I got along with Anubis very well. He was my best friend and soon upgraded to "friends with benefits" and we had a few flings, but I suspected he desired more of a relationship than I was ready for.

We lived together in that place for over a year. Our apartment was extremely well warded, but still very spiritually active. Shadows would occasionally pass through the apartment but were frequently spotted on the porch, in the yard, lurking in the bushes. I felt watched, targeted, hunted...

AZAZEL began attacking Anubis. I would see him sitting there quietly, when suddenly his face would begin twitching and he would say he saw bright lights like flash bulbs strobing in the corner of the room... then he would get really tense as if he was in great pain or fighting off a seizure... and about twenty minutes later he would be completely exhausted.

"Azazel tried to take me over, but I was able to fight him off... he kept showing me images of all the things he wanted me to do to you... sick horrible things... it was so bad I can't even tell you about them."

This happened on three different occasions, and Anubis successfully fought him off each time. Eventually, Azazel realized Anubis was someone he could never possess and gave up trying. I never found out what visions he showed him. A decade has passed since then and he still refuses to tell me.

I had known Tim for some time. He was an Italian bodybuilder type who wore cool costumes to the goth clubs and was always very nice to everyone. We had been talking spiritual shit the past few weekends at the club, while drinking heavily. I could tell something was inside him... a major player.

"I'm **JIBRIL**," he said, offhandedly. I was in shock. Motherfucking Gabriel! Visions began popping through my mind. We used to ride together thousands of years ago. GABRIEL, UZAZIEL, AZAZEL, CASSIUS, YETAREL, and a few other heavy hitters. I see flashes of painted horses, swords, circular yurtlike cottages, people being initiated into our army with a branding iron, and lots of snow. Gabriel was our Captain. Suddenly, I was back in line at the club. I blinked twice.

"I am **UZAZIEL**," I said. He nodded.

"That's cool." It was a profound experience, finally meeting another Brethren from the old crew... someone just like me. We hugged and the energy was so powerful everyone around us felt a shockwave and heard a noise like a bass drum "but played in reverse" if that makes sense. Everyone took several steps away from us, confused by what just happened. Suze looked at us wide eyed and just said "WOW." I wasn't drunk enough for this, so I ordered another glassful of *Black Magic*.

That night I let him take me home. I had found my Captain. He was my boyfriend now.

I was still living with Anubis, but had been spending a lot of time with Tim. One night I got an unexpected phone call from Anubis.

He was dating a sweet quiet girl named Pamela who had some psychic ability. She would read tarot cards and palms, but we didn't realize she had other abilities and apparently neither did she. She had suddenly had a fit, fallen into a trance, then began channeling a spirit... violently.

Anubis had been visiting at her house when suddenly her face contorted and her voice changed, becoming a feral snarl, as she began yelling profanity and threats while demanding to talk to me. I barely knew the girl.

"Queen... I have an emergency over here. I think Pamela is possessed by Azazel and I don't know what to do."

"LET ME TALK TO THAT CUNT!!!" she screamed in the background.

"Put her on the phone," I said. It wasn't her anymore. AZAZEL had taken complete control. We had an interesting chat that lasted about twenty minutes. She told me a number of very personal secrets about my life that neither Pamela or Anubis had any way of knowing... then she began talking about my past lives. She described how he had slaughtered my family in one life and tortured me to death in two others, then flatly stated that he intended to kidnap me, chain me up in a cave, and spend a week raping me while cutting off various body parts and eating them.

Eventually I got Anubis back on the phone. He sounded frightened. I told him I could not make it out there tonight and it would be unsafe for me to be in the same room as her, so I would give him instructions. I had him burn one of her sage wands, then take some salt and make the seal of **MARCHOSIAS** on the floor, then use oil to draw his sigil over the doors and windows. While the line was open I began chanting until I went into trance and began speaking in tongues.

A half hour later, Anubis told me she had gone into convulsions before finally falling into a deep restful sleep.

"You're welcome," I said, and hung up.

112

Tim told me he had a Middle-Eastern friend named Shalome
who had been teaching him locksmithing and was having serious
problems with being pressured by an intrusive entity. He asked if
I could meet with him to see what could be done, and I agreed,
making arrangements to meet in a neutral park at noon the next
day.

Shalome was a swarthy fellow with a thick accent who was very
polite. My reputation had preceded me and he showed proper
respect. All sorts of red flags went up when he told me he'd been
having visions of an entity with red and yellow eyes flickering like
fire who had been "putting thoughts in his head to make him
crazy."

I had him shuffle the cards and laid them out for a reading. They
clearly indicated that something very powerful and non-human
was bearing down on him. Then he told me, "I think I heard him
say his name... does Azazel mean anything to you?"

I quickly collected the cards and put the deck pack in the box. "I
cannot help you. That is a long time enemy of mine who has
attacked me several times and I have no power to protect you
from that one. I am sorry." He was absolutely distraught, but I
suddenly felt vulnerable and unsafe. He was clearly unbalanced
and Azazel could easily jump into him at any moment and
murder me. I left very quickly.

Shortly thereafter, Shalome lost his mind and flipped out on both
Tim and Anubis causing them to cut off all further contact with

him. He dropped off the radar immediately afterwards and disappeared. I have no idea what happened to him.

113

For New Year's Eve, myself and Tim were invited to a house party at the home of a mutual friend. It was BYOB so I brought a handle of rum. There were snacks and a DJ was playing a mix of Industrial and Punk. Only about thirty people showed up, mostly folks I recognized from the club, and overall there was a relaxed mellow vibe. Everyone was having a nice time.

I had been sitting at the kitchen table with some of my magickal friends having a conversation about, of all things, spiritual boundaries and shielding ourselves from negative energies. We had each had a drink or two, but none of us were intoxicated. One of my best friends, Nick, was an energy worker who practiced *Reiki*, and he said that he didn't know how to form a proper shield and tended to absorb other people's bad energy, soaking it up like a sponge. I offered to try drawing some of the bad energies out of him, after which one of the others would instruct him in the fundamentals of white light shielding.

I began chanting, and he said he felt things like heavy weights being pulled out of him, one after another. He was glad to be rid of them and felt lighter and lighter... then his eyes began twitching and he fell out of his chair.

Years later, he told me that once he was clean, he was immediately entered by an angry male entity that was somehow connected to me who felt like an abusive ex... but at that moment he completely blacked out.

I asked him if he was okay, concerned he might be having some sort of seizure. He began mumbling in a low pitched garbled voice before suddenly shouting profanities at me... but through clenched teeth, making it difficult to make out all the words. I needed to lean in closer when he lunged, trying to grab me, and the two witches held him down while he thrashed on the floor, making a hell of a racket as he kicked at the table and chairs. Soon, curious onlookers began wandering over to the kitchen and Tim needed to block the doorway to keep them out.

Suddenly, Nick locked eyes with me and growled, **"I'm going to rape you! I want to rape you just like I did in the bayou, Vicki!"** Everyone recoiled back as if rocked by some sort of invisible shock wave, then they collectively looked at him and gasped because it was so unbelievable. Nick was the kindest, gentlest, sweetest person we knew... it was not possible these hateful things were coming from his mouth.

"Did he just say that?" one of the witches said, looking to me.

"It wasn't him. That is not Nick." He looked right at me and *smirked,* before ranting and raving about all the horrible things he wanted to do to me while referring to my Victorian name in the same way Devon used to. I realized then that Azazel had taken him, and I was unable to exorcize Azazel. I glanced over at Tim, who looked scared.

"I think we need to leave now," he said. I agreed. And as quickly as it took him over, Azazel departed. Nick sat up, looking dazed and confused, having no recollection of what had just transpired. A mob of upset people collected outside the kitchen, drawn by the noise, demanding to see what was going on. The mellow relaxed vibe of the party had turned toxic. A couple of drunk guys tried to push past Tim and were shoved back, then he took my hand and pulled me through the crowd until we were outside.

"That was really fucked up," I said, shaken by the revelation that Azazel had been acting through the driver who assaulted me in Louisiana.

"It followed us out here... we need to go!" he said. We ran to his car, a little *RAV 4,* and took off.

Nick used to be one of my best friends. We used to hang out all the time. He would call me up and ask if I wanted to go shopping or get lunch and not once did he ever flirt with me or say anything untoward or inappropriate. He was one of the nicest people I knew, and I later heard that he was shocked and horrified by what had happened... but after Azazel has possessed someone once it becomes far easier for him to do it a second time. Out of necessity, I distanced myself from him, as well as that entire group of friends, because I was scared. Yes, big bad Queen was scared.

It was a one time thing. Azazel only used him for a few moments to send that one hateful message like a slap across the face. He told me that when he snapped out of trance the expression on my face was terrified, as if I had just seen my worst nightmare, and he knew that he had done something horrible. I am so sorry, Nick... you didn't deserve to be shut out of my life like that... it wasn't your fault.

114

Every time I visited Tim's apartment I was inexplicably drawn to a rock he kept on a shelf. It was a tektite, a meteor fragment shaped like a huge orange wedge, but the inside was covered with crystals like a geode. It looked like Superman's house. Every time I picked it up I wanted to hug it.

The second time I picked it up, one of the crystals popped off in my hand. Tim was shocked. He said that hundreds of people had handled that meteorite and it had been dropped on the ground several times and no chips or pieces had ever come off of it.

After considering all the problems I'd been having with Azazel, and how much I loved that rock, he told me "I feel like you should hold onto this for a little while... maybe it can help protect you."

I loved that rock. Every day I would hug it and pet it. I would sleep with it next to me in my bed at night. I could not understand my fascination with this rock.

A month later, I was performing a ritual, cutting open my arm to use my blood to paint sigils on parchment. The meteorite was in my lap. Suddenly there was a sonic **_BOOM_** that made the entire house shake, and a dark shadow projected from the rock, took on a manlike form, then ran straight through the wall. "WHAT THE FUCK WAS THAT?" Anubis yelled from the next room as he ran to me.

I looked down. 2 drops of blood had fallen onto the crystals and spread throughout the matrix, leaving a dark red stain. I tried holding it under the sink, spraying water over it while scrubbing it with a toothbrush, but I couldn't clean it off. It was as if the blood had been sucked inside the crystals.

20 minutes later the phone rang. It was Tim. *"Where is the meteorite?"* he asked. He sounded afraid.

"It's right here."

"What did you do to the meteorite?"

"Ummm... I cut myself and accidentally got a drop of blood on it... then we heard a big boom and a shadow ran through the wall." He went quiet for a few moments.

"Shit. I'll call you back." Then he hung up. I sat there, looking at the handset. Nope, that wasn't mysterious at all. What the fuck did you give me, Tim?

115

Everything changed between me and Tim after that. He became very withdrawn, sullen, depressed... he began drinking a lot more and didn't want to hang out as much.

He told me that a few years earlier he had been working with the *Goetia* and summoned **BAAL**. I never got the details, but apparently they did not get along at all, Baal kept trying to kill him, and somehow Tim managed to trap him inside the meteorite... which for some reason he then decided to give to me.

He said that as soon as Baal was released he immediately went after him and began throwing things around his room. I went over there and attempted to make peace between them, negotiate a truce, diplomatically stating that it was all a misunderstanding and they should agree to have no further contact. Eventually, Baal agreed to leave Tim alone. I worked with Baal a few times after that with no problems, me and him seem to get along fine.

Tim isolated himself and stopped going out to the clubs. He sent me a few texts about how depressed he was, then called me on the phone to announce he was breaking up with me.

I was utterly devastated. We had been together 5 months and unlike Ray and Aaron, he was the first man I'd ever truly loved. I had finally found someone just like me who I shared a past timeline with and he just threw me away like I was nothing! My life felt like it was spinning out of control. I felt completely dead inside. My chest hurt.

A few weeks later, myself and Anubis went to a "Psychic Fair" event, and I decided to visit the Kirlian photography booth to have an alleged photo of my aura taken and analyzed. The psychic looked at my photo and said nothing... she just hugged me. She was crying. I looked down at the photograph. There was an angry red blotch right over my heart. "You need to put this breakup behind you or you are literally going to die... your heartstrings are snapping one after another." I had told her nothing about my breakup and the constant chest pain. I'd told her nothing at all.

The next morning I woke up and tasted ashes. I felt completely numb. Anubis still had not gotten home from work. Robotically, I felt compelled to pick up the razor sharp combat knife I use for ritual. I walked out of my bedroom, across the living room, and into the spare room we used for storage.

I knelt down on the floor. Turning the blade towards myself, I centered the point just beneath my breastbone and pushed it through my cotton tank top, pulling it deeper, feeling the blade part flesh as it sunk in about half an inch... I was about to throw myself forward, slamming my bodyweight down as the pommel struck the carpeted floor, hammering the 7" blade all the way into my chest and through my heart. "WHAT THE FUCK ARE YOU DOING?" Anubis shouted, as he ran forward and snatched the knife away from me. I had not heard him come home. I was unable to explain myself... I felt half asleep, entranced, like walking through a dream.

Things became very strained after that. Anubis was hurt deeply that I had chosen Tim over him, and the suicide he interrupted was just too much for him to take. I realized I'd be needing to find another place to stay soon.

116

My chest continued to hurt. I was depressed and drinking too much. I needed a change.

I started dating a DJ who was heavy into the Industrial scene and would always dress in the cyber goth style, which I thought was cool at the time. He was a bit of a womanizer but said he wanted to date me exclusively... which of course ended up meaning I was expected to be exclusive to him, but not vice versa.

One night I noticed he had something inside him, an entity which made him so confident and extroverted, but drove him to other behaviors as well. As I slept, the entity revealed himself to me on the Astral as **MALPHAS.**

The next day, I spoke to him about it, and he was well aware of the spirit. He said that sometimes he wished it wasn't there. "I can help you get rid of it if you want reprieve," I said. He told me he'd give it some thought.

That night, while sleeping beside him, I woke up to him choking me with both hands. His eyes were completely black. The chokehold was not applied correctly and I laughed in his face. "Is that all you got, bitch? You're gonna have to do better than that!" His eyes cleared and went back to normal, he looked shocked. I rolled over and went back to sleep.

A few weeks later, at the Halloween Ball, I was dressed up as Sugar Bear, the Juggalo Pimp from the *ICP* movie *Big Money Hustlas,* having a great time. I needed to talk to him and interrupted while he was talking to some cute blonde in a skimpy outfit. Annoyed, he shoved me... in my club, at the biggest event of the year, in front of all my friends. Everyone saw it. I was humiliated. I left and never talked to that motherfucker again.

I hated that motherfucker, and considered him an enemy for years. He moved to the Springs so I rarely ran into him, but last year he walked into my club and saw me. He stalked away. I noticed him glaring at me from a distance a few times that night, but he never approached... he just drank more drinks and got madder and madder.

Finally, I decided I needed to do something about this. I do not like having an enemy walking around in my club. He was standing in line at the bar and I walked right up to him, smiled, and extended my hand. He looked down at it. "Really?" I smiled wider and nodded. He took my hand and shook it, then smiled himself. "Cool." It seemed like a huge weight had been lifted from him.

There are many ways to deal with your enemies. Diplomacy is one of the very best ways. Remember that.

117

I loved working at *Fusion Federation* on the Mall. It was owned by three Asian ladies who treated us like family and wanted us to focus on making sure every customer had a wonderful shopping experience and walked out with an outfit that suited them perfectly, and if they bought a corset they needed to know exactly how to put it on themselves. That was a lot more important to them than high pressure sales. I took a lot of pride in my work, even though it didn't pay very well.

It was a very popular shop that brought in a lot of business. We had customers who would save up all year to come there during an annual convention and spend thousands. Many regular customers would shop there almost weekly. It was a shock when the Mall canceled our lease so a shitty barbeque chain restaurant could have our space. We were all given a week to move out.

I relocated to their Belmar shop, but it wasn't the same crowd as at the 16th Street Mall, just a bunch of boring locals, and the Boulder shop was nothing but snotty, hoity toity rich fucks. It was awful, it wasn't fun anymore, and it was a very long commute.

I put out some feelers and heard about a job opening at *Broadridge Financial* as a "stock transfer agent," which is a clerk who processes all the legal paperwork required to transfer stocks to another party.

With my references and experience I was immediately hired. It paid significantly better than *Fusion Federation* with opportunities for bonuses and promotions. I had found a new career.

118

A friend of a friend had just gone through a horrible divorce and was in dire need of a roommate to share expenses at her new apartment... and that was how I met Sarah.

Sarah was a wonderful girl, absolutely the best roommate I've ever had. Most of my former roommates were slobs who never did dishes or picked up after themselves, but she was a regular Suzie Homemaker and our place was always orderly and spotless. She also was an amazing cook, and even if the refrigerator was empty she could go through the cupboard, pull out a few forgotten boxes and cans, and whip together a gourmet 5 course dinner. I was in continuous awe of her culinary abilities.

Unlike most goths, she was not pagan... she was Christian, but not the devout or judgmental type. She knew I was pagan and was very open-minded about my beliefs, which she understood were somewhat dark.

One day she came to me and said, "I know you're into some things and that's okay, but Queen, I'm really scared... I keep waking up and seeing a shadow standing at the foot of my bed." I considered who that might be, closed my eyes, opened my Third Eye, and scanned the area of her room. I saw exactly who she was talking about.

"Oh, you don't need to be scared of that one... he's just checking in on you and making sure you're safe."

"Oh... well, that's kinda creepy... but okay." And that was pretty much all that was said about my spiritual practices the entire year we lived together.

119

I met Butcher at the club. He was a self taught musical genius who could play any stringed instrument beautifully, even new types he'd never held before, and made it look easy. He composed veritable symphonies, and on the rare occasions he performed a live concert he would take pains to demonstrate to each musician exactly how he wanted their instrument played.

For some bizarre reason he never released an album, even though he had plenty of opportunity to do so. He generally only played at local Death Metal events. I called him Butcher because his day job was working as a master meatcutter for a supermarket.

Aside from being a brilliant musician whose talent I was in awe of, there wasn't much noteworthy about Butcher. He was very introverted and softspoken, and even though he was heavily invested in the Satanic Black Metal scene, there really didn't seem to be anything dark about him at all. He was actually very nice, innocent really... I think he may've been on the autism spectrum.

He told me he was having "really fucked up dreams" and images about me that "someone was putting in his head" but, like Anubis, he refused to tell me. He would wake up ashen, pale, shaken. Eventually I told him I had a nemesis, and it was an entity, and it was dangerous. He puffed up and stated he'd protect me by "kicking his ass." I looked at him and blinked. Sure you will, sweetie...

Everything seemed fine between us. He even bought me a 5 string bass guitar and invited me to jam with him in the studio space he rented. We played together for a few months, just the two of us... then he started inviting his friend Bambi to listen to us. She didn't play an instrument. She was a stripper.

On Valentine's Day, he surprised me by bringing home two thick filet mignon steaks cut into the shape of hearts... then he asked if I minded if Bambi joined us for dinner because she had been "going through some shit." I thought that was odd, but said okay. A little while later he asked if I might be into a threesome. I paused to rewind what I thought I just heard him ask me.

"I don't know how I feel about that," I said, which should've been a hint that I wasn't cool with it, at least not on short notice on motherfucking Valentine's Day.

Anyway, I totally did not feel like it at all after watching him lovingly split his steak with her. Nobody had any sex, but he ended up spooning her all night, totally ignoring me. I was livid.

The next morning I demanded he drive me home. Bambi sat in the back seat with a wide grin on her face the whole way. A few days later he dumped me, and I found out he'd been boning her for weeks. That whole while she'd been pretending to be my friend. It was like a double betrayal, and it was so unexpected. It hurt me a lot.

120

I met Jonathan at the club. He was in a band with a friend I knew for years who introduced us and vouched for him. He was built like a fireplug, solid muscle, with a shaved head and had been part of the scene for a while but we'd never met. He was very charming and had an unusual accent, which he claimed was Botswanan.

After closing, we walked together to *Tom's Diner* on Colfax for breakfast. We were both somewhat drunk, and the whole way there he kept alluding to various spiritual topics but was being frustratingly vague. I started to speak about my own experiences and he cut me off with a statement that made my blood run cold. "I know you have a story, but you do not need to tell it to me. I think you should know that Azazel is good and his heart is in nature, and I do not want to hear you say anything bad about him because of what he did for me." Then he began rambling about a time he was up a tree, sawing branches, when his safety line broke and he felt that Azazel saved his life.

I was completely numb. Aside from Anubis and Tim, neither of whom had spoken to me for months, no-one in Denver knew anything about my nemesis Azazel. This man claimed alliance with my Enemy. I was done running. I cared not about consequences. I needed to learn his secrets.

This meeting occurred at a very low point in my life. I had no-one I could confide in and felt completely isolated and unprotected. I began questioning my sanity, thinking that maybe Aaron had been right all along and these were nothing but imaginings and delusions. Then this turd gets dropped in my lap. This turd smelled like VALIDATION.

I knew from the very beginning that this was a set up, a glamour, a trap set by the Enemy. I did not care. I was probably just going to kill myself anyway, convinced I was crazy. Everyone at the club called me "Crazy Queen" for my penchant of getting shitfaced, ranting about stupid monkeys, then headbutting brick walls while screaming or crying. No, instead I intended to face my Enemy head on...

One evening, while Jonathan was visiting me at the apartment I shared with Sarah, I lit an incense stick... then turned to see his eyes glowing electric blue, his aura bright blue flames. The name **KANAAN** rang out in my head. I shut my eyes for a few moments, then reopened them to see him smirking at me. "What? *What did you see?"* he asked, waiting.

"Nothing."

"Are you sure?"

"Yes... what was I supposed to see?" He grimaced, frustrated.

He tried this same trick, followed by the exact same words, several times over the next few weeks. I feigned ignorance, playing it cool, waiting it out to see what I might learn.

Sara received notification from property management that the building had been sold and rent under the new owners was going to double. Rather than renewing the lease, she decided to move in with her boyfriend.

Jonathan shared his small 1 bedroom apartment with an ex girlfriend, so moving in with him wasn't even an option, and I had lost contact with Anubis. I asked around and there was no-one else I wanted to share an apartment with, so I needed to find a new place on my own.

Soon, I found a studio apartment in a complex at Evans and Quebec, a mile away from Jonathan's place. There was nowhere to store my stuff so the walls were lined with cardboard boxes that were stacked to the ceiling. It was very claustrophobic.

There was a *Filter* concert at the *Ogden* I wanted to see. Jonathan was working and couldn't go, so I went with a few friends, right after work, wearing a black dress and platform boots.

The venue was mostly empty because *Filter* was the headliner who did not come on until at least an hour after the doors opened. People were slowly trickling in as the opening act, *Helmet*, played. There were only five people in the pit, just acting stupid running around in circles. We were not in the pit, we were off to the side of the stage, well out of the way of the stupidity.

My two friends went to the bar to get drinks, and as soon as they left, one of the jerks in the pit body slammed me elbow first, knocking me to the floor, before running off. I looked up and saw him, a gigantic Samoan looking motherfucker, at least 300#, with the sides of his head shaved, tennis shoes, khaki shorts, and a pink polo shirt... not the sort of thing people typically wear to these shows.

I struggled to get up when he came at me again, sprinting straight at me, leaping into the air and stomping on me with so much force he bounced off like a springboard... when the bone in my leg snapped it was so loud I could hear it above the music.

He turned and looked at me, a completely blank expression on his face with dull glazed eyes, before walking out of the venue. It was as if he paid for a ticket specifically to target me. I had no idea who he was, I had never seen him before in my life. The pain was excruciating. I began screaming. The people who were standing in front of me turned around, looked down at me scornfully for disrupting their concert experience, then turned back towards the stage.

My friends came back and were like, "What the fuck, Queen? We were gone for like five minutes!" They managed to remove my boot and my foot just flopped to the side, turned beet red, and instantly swelled up like a balloon. "Do you think you can walk on it?" One of them asked.

"Does it LOOK like I can walk on it, you retarded motherfucker?" I yelled. More people I knew came over, the bouncers ran over and one of them called an ambulance. I told them what the guy who attacked me looked like and they searched the entire venue, inside and out, and did not find him. A few people even walked the block and checked across the street. He had vanished.

A few minutes later the paramedics arrived and strapped me onto a gurney. Once we were in the ambulance they asked me to rate the pain on a scale of 1-10. I told them it was a 12. They injected me with Fetanyl and instantly the pain dissolved... in fact, I felt better than I'd ever felt in my life... I felt like doing cartwheels. "Yoo guyz are so cool! Yoo all deserve a raise!" I proclaimed. They unanimously agreed.

After getting my X-rays the young doctor came in to tell me he had great news. "What? My ankle's not broken?"

"Oh no... it's *really* broken... but it's SO COOL! None of us have ever seen a break like this before, even in the medical journals! We are going to put your case in the *Journal of the American Medical Association!* How did you manage to do this?"

"Ummm... I was wearing platform boots and was laying on the ground with my ankles crossed when this big guy jumped up and stomped on it with both feet."

"Oh... alright, that explains it. It is just so unusual for the bone in the back to break, and the way it broke was so odd, and the tendon completely tore free... you have insurance, right?" He suddenly looked concerned.

"I have Medicaid." His face immediately brightened again.

"That's wonderful! Don't worry, we'll do a great job fixing you up. Every doctor in the country will see our work! Thank you for coming in today!"

"Ummm... are you going to name this break after me? Do I get royalties or some shit?"

"No... but I can hook you up with a CD-ROM of the X-rays."

Somehow, I wasn't nearly as excited about this as everyone else was.

124

For the first time in my life, I felt completely helpless. I was in constant agony and could barely move around my apartment to shower or feed myself. It was humiliating.

Jonathan brought me over a battered grimy toaster oven he thought would be helpful and would only visit for a couple of hours every Sunday now.

I had found a big chunk of Labradorite in my old things which I placed prominently upon my altar. The next time Jonathan came over he winced a bit, then took my hand and said "When I'm here, you need to put that Labradorite away... it really bothers me" but refused to say why.

Occasionally he would take me to the club and wander off to talk to other girls all night while I hobbled around on my crutches and got smashed mixing rum with my pain medication.

One night, *Aesthetic Perfection* was playing at *Casselman's*, and I was really looking forward to seeing them. Three drinks later, I see Butcher and his whore Bambi. I do not recall my exact words... in fact, I have limited recollection of the event in question, but apparently I flung a glass of rum in his face, headbutted a brick wall several times, then went outside on the smoking patio to yell and cry for about 20 minutes until someone told Jonathan what I was doing and he came out to take me home, berating me the whole while for "embarrassing" him and making him miss the show.

After I broke my ankle, I learned who my real friends were. Back when I was laughing and happy and throwing cash around like a drunken sailor, *everyone* wanted to be Queen's friend. But when I was depressed, broken, broke... everyone turned their back on me. No-one called, no-one visited, no-one offered to help... except my friend Tammy and her boyfriend Joe, they were the only ones who would check in to see how I was doing, occasionally bringing over food or taking me out of the house for awhile. None of the other hundred people in the scene who claimed to be my friend seemed to give a shit about me now.

While I was home alone, I was noticing some new and unusual spiritual activity. I began hearing strange noises: rustling, knocking, little running feet, whispering, giggling... it was as if my apartment had been infested with imps.

I was too tired and in too much pain after a day of work at the office to attempt managing an exorcism. I called up Jonathan to complain. After listening, he said "Hold on for a minute." A few minutes passed, then he came back on the line and said, "Okay, that should do it." I paused to listen... the constant scuffling and chattering had stopped. It was completely silent.

"What did you do? I asked.

"They're all over here now." I honestly did not know what to say to that. How could he possibly have managed that without a pre-existing connection? The only explanation is that he must've sent them to spy on me, and when they got bored they became rambunctious.

That suspicion was confirmed one night, after he had a few drinks, when he carelessly admitted that he'd been watching me for two years, waiting to make his move. Really? When was that? "I used to ride behind you everyday on the bus." My blood ran cold. It was him all along.

I needed to make this call several more times over the next few months, and every single time he did the exact same thing, and the noises would stop. With all the weird creepy shit I've had happen in my life, the imp incidents are near the top of that list.

Jonathan met me at *Leela's* before the *Combichrist* concert at the "Ominous" event at *Tracks.* I had been looking through old boxes for my outfit and found a ring I had forgotten about. It was Labradorite... and I had also forgotten his prior comment about the Labradorite on my altar.

He sat down across from me, reached under the table, closed his hand over mine and said, "You know that's not going to keep me away, right? I'm not going to turn you over... I'm not going to take you to them." Then he smiled, stood, and we walked out to the car to go to the show.

Shortly after we arrived, some girl I'd never seen before walked up, glared at me for several moments, then said "Oh... so *you're* the one." Before spinning on her heel and stomping away.

Confused, I looked to Jonathan for an explanation. For some reason he looked scared, as if I'd caught him doing something wrong. "Oh, it's nothing... she's just this crazy girl I didn't want to date so she's been stalking me." I was unconvinced, but said nothing.

I was friends with one of the event promoters, and he was considerate and thoughtful enough to set out a reserved sofa for me that was cordoned off. While we were sitting there, during an intermission in the concert, I decided to quiz him to see how he answered. "Do any of these names mean anything to you?" Then I proceeded to say four names, including the one I believed was his, but deliberately mispronouncing it as "Canin."

His features immediately clouded, beetle brow crinkling, as he stared straight ahead, not looking at me, as he slowly and deliberately spoke through gritted teeth. "His name is **KANAAN**... spelled K A N A A N... and do not say it again unless you want to see him." Then he stormed off to get a drink.

He avoided me for the rest of the night and was quiet the whole drive back to my apartment.

I had been working very hard at *Broadridge* all year long in hope of a raise and promotion. Instead it was given to a far less qualified and less experienced girl who had only been there a few months.

Apparently, she'd been having an affair with one of the managers, then walked into the operations manager's office and literally *cried,* begging for the promotion, asserting how much she *needed* the extra money.

They announced she had gotten the job and congratulated her, like she had done something to actually earn it. She was all smiles and everyone in the office applauded. Everyone except me. That was *my* promotion which she *stole* from me.

I picked up the phone and called *Knight Transportation.* They offered me my old job back at 45 cents per mile, which came out to about $1,200 a week after taxes, significantly more than she would be making as my new supervisor. Then I cleaned out my desk and quit.

Jonathan was so happy to hear I was going back on the road. That was going to free up his Sundays to see other bitches.

I had been hearing from friends that Jonathan had been spotted visiting other girls' apartments during the day, and notorious skank Kimmy Drippy was bragging that he rawdogged her in a graveyard. I was horrified. After the first two months we'd been together I thought we were exclusive... and we'd stopped using protection. Well, that explained the urinary tract infections. Now I needed to get tested for STDs.

Fortunately, the tests came back clean, but I cut him off completely as soon as I found out. I also found out he'd been lying about working long hours too... in fact, he no longer was even employed at that restaurant. The next time I went over to his apartment to pick him up, I saw him walking arm in arm with another girl. As they came closer, I saw it was his ex-girlfriend platonic roommate. "Oh HI!" she said, "I'm sure you've heard *all* about me!" she gushed. Actually, no, I hadn't. I looked in her innocent dimwitted eyes and realized she didn't even know he'd been my boyfriend for the past seven months, and certainly didn't know about the half dozen other bitches I'd heard about... she thought she was the only one too.

Later that evening, he told me his new job would be requiring a lot of travel, so he didn't feel it was "viable" to continue our relationship any longer and dumped me. I think it was probably in large part because he suspected people had been telling me he'd been cheating... after all, Kimmy Drippy had even posted about it on *Facebook*. He knew he couldn't hide it any longer.

Afterwards, he tried to damage my credibility by besmirching my reputation, spreading rumors that I was "manipulative and abusive" to him, before messaging all the local girls on my *Facebook* friend list... most of whom he'd never actually met before, to warn them I was "crazy" and troll for sympathy for all the times I allegedly "embarrassed him with my behavior." He even went so far as to tell Sarah, "The only reason I helped her was because she was making me look bad gimping around with her broken ankle." A bunch of them sent me screenshots, asking me who the fuck this creep was. Gaslighting FAIL, dipshit.

129

I spent several evenings meditating upon the events of the past seven months, all the things Jonathan said, all the things he did...

Admitting to stalking me for two years, riding behind me on the bus all those times I felt Azazel's presence, then swooping in at my most vulnerable, after losing contact with Anubis and being dumped by Tim and Butcher.

Upon our very first meeting, declaring himself a devoted servant of Azazel and flatly stating not to bother telling him my story because he already knew it.

Repeatedly trying to impress me by puffing up before my clairvoyant sight, revealing the distinctive blue flamed aura of a *djiin*.

Demonstrating and declaring an aversion to Labradorite, a stone known to protect against *djinn*.

The inexplicable appearance of imps in my apartment which seemed to be under his direct control.

Correctly articulating and spelling the name Kanaan, which flashed in my head during his elaborate demonstrations.

Stating "I will not turn you over to them," as if he had been assigned that specific task as his mission.

I realized that KANAAN was a *djinn* in the employ of AZAZEL and ASMODAI who had appeared in several of my lifetimes. He was Azazel's "Fetch" who always brought me to him. He was leading the men who slaughtered my German family before bringing me to Devon.

It all started flooding back...

I remembered it all.

130

That night, I dreamed of when I lived in Germany, hundreds of years ago, back in Victorian times. Coincidentally, my name then was Victoria.

I remembered servants coming into my cell to help bathe and dress me, and a stern matronly woman with dark hair tied back who silently stared at me the whole while.

Sometimes Devon would briefly take me out of the cell for a few hours. A few times we went upstairs to a wide banquet hall with a long table. I had strict instructions never to speak unless spoken to, but no-one ever did. Men and women sat around the table with Devon seated at the head. I never sat alongside him, but rather somewhere in the middle. The women at the table seemed self-assured, competent, powerful... I wished I could be more like them.

One day I was led into a chapel and surprisingly left alone. The domed ceiling had a detailed and realistic mural of deep space with gaseous nebulas, and near the center was a woman wrapped in scarves and veils... all different shades of blue... with fair skin and long black hair. Suddenly I realized the entire mural was moving, swirling, fulminating, with her scarves and hair billowing in a breeze. She gazed down upon me and said, "Child, don't you recognize what you are?"

Later, I was taken to a ritual chamber and chained to a slab, while the people I recognized from the banquet hall stood around me. Devon stood at my head, chanting, before slamming a dagger into my chest and ripping downwards, hoping to obtain some secret magickal instrument hidden within.

I woke up, not in my apartment but in my cell, still back in Victorian times. There was no mark on my flesh, it was all like a dream, but I knew it was not. I knew Devon had attempted to cut something out of me and I was not supposed to survive, but somehow things did not work out the way he had planned. I knew he would never give up, there would be other attempts, experiments, torture.

That was the day I found the knife... it was not a letter opener... it was a thin stiletto, designed to kill with a single thrust. It did not belong in my cell... someone had left it there, not for me, but to sabotage Devon's plans for me... to prevent him from obtaining the instrument...

131

My ankle had two huge screws in it, but it had healed up sufficiently enough for me to go back on the road again. I began driving for *Knight* the second time.

Knight paid well, but the trucks were limited to 67 mph and you only had a "bed heater" to keep you warm in the Winter which frequently did not work. The air conditioning only worked while the truck was running, but there was an idle limiter which would not allow the truck to run more than 5 minutes while parked unless it was at least 80 degrees outside, which was a huge pain in the ass... but not as bad as being expected to run around for hours looking for an empty trailer without compensation.

Truck driving is very boring and my only social contact was phone calls from a handful of friends, mostly other truckers, and *Facebook*. One evening, alone in my sleeper compartment, I jokingly posted a status update of "feelin frisky." The next morning I had a message in my inbox from someone who'd never messaged me before or commented on my posts, and I had no idea who he was because I did not recognize the name and he had posted no pics, but he lived in Denver, we had about a hundred mutual friends, and his profile pic was *Aegishjalmr*... the "Helm of Terror"... one of my most sacred symbols for many years with deep personal meaning.

I no longer have the original message, but the gist of it was, "I swear to respect you and treat you extremely well, and I will cook you breakfast in the morning." That was certainly a bold statement. Who the fuck is this motherfucker rockin *my* symbol saying he's gonna make me breakfast? He is probably another of Azazel's Assholes.

I dismissed him by saying I was very busy the next time I would be in town and unable to socialize for at least a month, maybe two, thinking that would be the end of it. He continued to message me regularly, far more often than any of my exes. Soon, we began talking on the phone.

Clint's voice was very soothing, and he was articulate and intelligent, but I saw he had mutual friends with Jonathan and they ran in some of the same circles, which raised a lot of red flags, so I needed to proceed with caution. I felt he was a being far more powerful than Kanaan. I did not know if he was friend or foe.

132

I had spoken to my old friend, Gimp, regarding his thoughts about this new fellow, and he told me that he seemed like a decent enough guy, better than most of the creeps I'd dated anyway. "Go for it, Sis... what've ya got to lose?"

He had a point. I'd been struggling with depression again and had been considering just giving up on dating, trucking, struggling, breathing. Everything had been turning to shit since I'd moved back to Denver, one slap in the face after another, and I was done. The future looked hopeless. I just wanted it to be over.

I agreed to let Clint take me out for an early dinner, not having any idea what to expect. If he turned out to be a total loser I could just bail and take an Uber home. If he turned out to be cool I had been given a pair of tickets to a show at the *Oriental Theater* later that evening.

I was all gothed out, with platform boots, fishnet tights, a miniskirt, and an assortment of black straps and buckles on my top. I had multiple spiked piercings in my face and long strands of thick blue yarn braided into my hair... then I put on my warpaint with a stripe down my chin.

He showed up wearing an untucked red Hawaiian shirt and an Irish flatcap. His right arm was black leather straps from elbow to wrist and terminated in a steel meathook. Immediately, I had a flashback to a drunken night at *Milkbar* years earlier when a friend yelled, "Queen! I found your pirate!" and pointed him out. I noticed he was there with a short dark haired girl and only spoke to him for a moment before rushing off. My next thought was, *"I am way too extreme for him... he's gonna hate me."*

He took me by the hand and walked me to his car, a black primed Toyota sedan that looked like something from a Mad Max film, and politely opened the door for me. He drove me to what he told me was his favorite restaurant, *Phoenician Kabob*, which he said was owned by his friend. We each had the lamb, and I was introduced to a strong licorice flavored drink called *Arak*, followed by an assortment of honey drenched *baklava*.

I decided to invite him to the show. It was a decadent burlesque festival called "Carnivale Sensuale" with magic acts and a cash bar. I had performed with many of the dancers before, and he had dated one of the girls in the freak show, so perhaps he wasn't as vanilla as I'd feared.

We drove back to Denver down Federal at about a hundred miles per hour, before turning onto 8th and slowing to about 80. We caught air a couple of times. I'd had a few rum drinks and the street lights overhead reminded me of something from a videogame as he flew along the centerline, ignoring red lights. "This reminds me of *Pole Position*," I said.

His apartment was part of a small brick house in Cap Hill. It was spotlessly clean and smelled of incense. The first thing I noticed was the framed *Degas* on the wall... "Men Fighting with Cudgels"... the same image he chose for the background of his profile. The next thing I noticed was the altar.

His fingers traced the bone wings tattooed on my back... the sigils... the seals. He did not ask me what they meant. As he held me, I gazed into his eyes and they changed... bright white halos blazed around his pupils in the candlelit bedroom. "You're looking at a Death Angel," he told me. "You're my woman now," he said.

The next morning he cooked me breakfast as promised and brought it to me in bed. It was the best home fries I'd ever had with three over medium eggs, blueberry sausages, and a wonderfully spicy Bloody Mary.

He was so sweet to me.

It felt like coming *home.*

133

There was something dark about him, but he seemed far more light than dark... and he made me feel safe. When he drove me back to my truck he had a gift for me... a stonecutter's hammer. "If anyone fucks with you on the road, just slam the spike into their head and their lights will go out like that, clean and quiet." I turned it over in my hands and examined it. It was short, with a rubberized grip, and I had no doubt a head strike would be positively lethal.

"Thank you," I said.

"You be safe, Blue," he said, renaming me due to my blue yarn dreads.

We talked on the phone everyday and he began sharing songs on my *Facebook* page and referring to me as his "Buttercup." People I knew were like, "Who the fuck is this guy?" but I didn't say much... I wasn't entirely sure myself... but I liked him.

He never talked much about his past, but I soon found out that he'd written a few books, mostly self defense related, but also a book on the occult and a novel. I found out that he was best friends with Jonathan's martial arts instructor, and *his* instructor as well. He had worked in security and private investigations for years, and was dealing with PTSD from multiple incidents back in Tidewater Virginia and rural upstate New York. He also had a black primed V8 trike and rode with *Bikers Against Child Abuse*. He seemed like a cool guy.

Later, he revealed that his father had worked for the Jersey mob and he was friends with guys in several outlaw motorcycle clubs and had alluded to some heavy shit a long time ago... his scars and ink backed that up. I looked at him with new eyes after that. He was *gangsta*... not like some punk ass gold chain wearin' bitch, but a genuine old skool Tommy gun gangsta. I knew this one would stand by my side and fight for me. I knew he would never back down from anyone or anything.

The next time I came into town, a face from my past had reached out via social media... a guy I hadn't seen since I was homeless on the streets, sleeping in the Silos. An unrelenting barrage of messages about how he was in town that week and intended to hunt me down because I was "his." I'd never even kissed this freak and had no idea why he suddenly had this obsession, but I knew he was batshit crazy and literally capable of anything. For one of the few times in my life, I was genuinely afraid.

I told Clint about him, and he used his investigative skills to pull his record and do a deep dive into his social media. "You ain't gonna believe this shit," he said. Apparently, this guy's job doing rigging for rock bands took him all over the country, and he had a thing for picking up homeless teenagers and bringing them back to his hotel room in every city he worked at. Googling his phone number brought up a recent male escort advertisement on *Backpage*: "I am giving it away for FREE!" with pics of him half nekkid and grinning on his motel bed. This was the guy who said he was coming for me and wouldn't take no for an answer, making threats when I told him to leave me alone. Several of his *Facebook* pics were of knives... big knives.

I had gotten back in touch with Anubis and called him for backup. We all met Downtown at *Double Daughters* and began drinking around noon, because that always helps. I noticed Clint's jacket seemed to hang differently, as if it was heavier than normal. "Check this shit out," he told Anubis, flicking open a huge double-serrated switchblade. "I have brought enough knives for everyone."

Five drinks later, some girl sat down next to Clint and began flirting with him. He pointed at me and told her I was his fiancée. "Oh, that's wonderful!" she gushed to me, "Can I see your ring?"

"I don't have a ring," I said, annoyed. "I *hate* diamonds." She nodded.

"Well, if you could have any stone you wanted, what would it be?"

Totally pissed, I spat, *"Black Pearl!"* and stormed off.

Later that evening, we walked into the club heavily armed and shitfaced drunk... then immediately began slamming doubles of *Ketel One* vodka, which I called "War Water." It was the first time Clint had been to this club. He didn't go out much and it showed.

As the night progressed, he yelled at two people and offered to gut another for "disrespecting" me... all of whom were easily twice his size... then walked over to a metal pole and repeatedly smashed his hook into it, ringing it like a bell as sparks flew. When I went over to get another drink, Suze looked over at him and said, "He reminds me of you."

The bad guy never showed, which was certainly for the best. After twelve vodkas, I had absolutely no doubt Clint would've murdered him on camera in front of a hundred witnesses, zero fucks given. Even Anubis was scared of him once he was in his cups. He was barely human when he was drunk, more like an Irish wolverine in a skin suit... yet he remained unfailingly polite to me.

The next morning, he made me breakfast in bed again. I was still drunk, and grateful for the Bloody Mary.

We went for a ride on the trike later, miles down Colfax and up past Red Rocks. On the way back, Lakewood Police clocked us doing about 70 in a 40. "Hold on," Clint told me. He wasn't joking. I nearly flew off when we took a sidestreet on 2 wheels, then made a rapid series of quick turns before flying down Wadsworth to Evans. We didn't get a ticket.

The next day, as he was driving me back to my truck, I was deep in thought about something, when suddenly I heard him flatly state, *"I love you."* It was so unexpected it hit me like a slap in the face. I choked up for a moment before composing myself.

"I believe words have power, and that is not a word to throw around lightly. Be very careful with that word." He looked at me for a few moments, taking in my reaction, saying nothing.

When we arrived at the *Knight* terminal he handed me something. "I wore this ring for ten years and kept it in my medicine bag for five... I want you to wear it now." It was a silver Celtic knotwork ring almost exactly like one I wore on the streets for years, then lost in one of my many moves. It was a size too big, but I felt a powerful magnetic charge sticking it to my ring finger... it wasn't coming off easily.

"Thank you," I said. Then he kissed me and gave me one of his switchblades as well, the secret agent kind that snaps out the front. He called it a Microtech.

"You be safe, Blue," he told me.

134

The next time I came home we had a nice time riding the trike, going out for sushi, then going to the club. We got a bit tipsy at the club.

Afterwards, we came directly home. Something seemed odd about Clint. He seemed extremely tense and very sober all of a sudden. There was a high intensity flashlight attached to his keys which he shone down the alley and into the bushes alongside the driveway. "Something feels off... it feels like we're walking into an ambush... stay behind me, and wait a moment before going into the apartment." I also felt it... a heavy pressure, like someone staring at the back of my head... through crosshairs.

He held open my door, helped me out, then shined the light towards his back porch. "Stay about five paces back," he said. He was hyperalert as he walked to the door, then proceeded to clear the small apartment. "It's okay, come inside, quick." After he locked the door, he apologized. "I'm so sorry... I just got the oddest feeling that something followed us home from the club tonight."

I sat down on one of the chairs in his livingroom. "There's something I need to tell you about me. I have a nemesis... and it's an entity. Have you ever heard of Azazel?"

That led to a long half drunk conversation that lasted until nearly 4 AM. I told him about my past lives, I told him about the relentless persecution, I told him I had a spirit inside me and it was a fallen angel. He listened, very patiently, somewhat skeptically, as if he was humoring me and somewhat annoyed about it.

"Alright... what is the angel's Name?"

"I am **UZAZIEL**," I said. The energy in the room immediately changed, as if a switch had been thrown.

"What???" he said... the word sounded choked... the expression on his face looked horrified. I didn't know what to make of that... I couldn't read him at all.

"Uzaziel," I repeated.

He fell to his knees and placed his head in my lap. I didn't know what to expect, but it certainly wasn't that. He looked up at me, earnestly, with tears in his eyes. *"I have been searching for you for so long!"*

I, too, had been searching for the one who would instantly recognize me and react in that very way.

This is the one I'd been waiting for.

135

The next morning, he told me he had a book I needed to read. "I wrote this for you," he said, telling me it would provide a few of the missing pieces to the puzzle.

He gave me yet another knife when he dropped me off at the terminal... a finger claw neck knife based on the Perrin *LaGriffe*, which he told me was the best self defense knife ever made. He was always giving me knives. "You be safe, Blue," he said.

The next chance I had, I began reading *The Outrider*. It was ostensibly a dark urban fantasy novel about widespread demonic possession amongst the street people of Denver and a war between several spiritual factions.

The first thing I noticed was that one of the main characters was possessed by the fallen angel Usiel, which is an alternate spelling of Uzaziel... and the character's human name was "BOB," which was a bogus name I frequently used on the street and it was part of a longstanding inside joke. Shocked, I read further.

He wrote about all the places I used to hang out at: *Milkbar*, the Silos, the Platte, the plains out East... he wrote about a character like Attitude, with his duster and khukri... he mentioned Asmodai several times, clearly referring to him as an enemy. So much of what he wrote coincided exactly with my own life. It was as if he was writing this book about *me!*

If I had randomly found this book somewhere and read it, I would've needed to track the author down to ask him how he knew so much about me. I had trouble putting it down. I read the whole thing in two nights... then I began reading it again. I couldn't believe it.

I talked to him on the phone about it. He told me he had the idea for the book over a decade ago, while he was still in Tidewater, but Virginia Beach certainly was not the appropriate setting so the project went on a back burner indefinitely. After moving to Denver he realized this was the perfect setting for his story.

He claimed he only loosely adhered to the original plot and characters and the book literally wrote itself, downloaded via automatism. He would go into trance and type nonstop for half a day, then look down at a near perfect rough draft written in a style that was not his using words he did not recognize.

He would always begin writing by sticking to a loose blueprint, and added a few elements in the final edit, reflecting his own personal experiences... the end result was more truth than fiction, but novelization is the best way to convey certain arcane topics so they are more easily digested and assimilated.

That book changed everything... profoundly. It completely removed any and all doubts I might've had.

The next time I came home, Clint got down on his knees in front of me again. He handed me a small hinged box. It was the biggest Black Pearl I'd ever seen, in a swirling white gold setting. He said it was an antique from Hawaii, handcrafted by a master jeweler and the only one of its kind. The size was 7.5... a perfect fit.

"You're mine now," he told me.

"Yes," I agreed.

Later that evening I posted a pic of both rings on my hand, changing my *Facebook* status to "Married" and saying simply, *"There is a lot you do not know, and that is as it should be. We are happy."*

I got far more "likes" than anything I'd ever posted before in my life.

In Colorado, all you need do to be common law married is simply announce your status publically, cohabitate, and present yourself as a married couple. No ceremony, court, or official documents required.

I remained on the road, coming back home every month. Most of my belongings were moved from my shoebox apartment to a storage unit, and the rest were kept in a closet and dresser at Clint's place.

Clint was always very happy to pick me up at the terminal. We would go to his friend's restaurant for lunch, and a variety of Chinese, Mexican, and sushi restaurants the rest of my brief stay. He requested those weekends off well in advance from his three jobs so he could take me to *Milkbar, Church*, and *3 Kings*. He always treated me with respect and never talked down to me or tried to impose his will upon me. He told me *we were a team.* None of my exes had ever treated me like an equal before.

We made plans to get officially married, with a ceremony and a marriage license. The date would be a year after our original announcement.

We began discussing spiritual matters more often and he was the only one who ever fully understood who I was and where I was coming from, even more so than Anubis, Serpent, Jabril. Like Jabril and Azazel, we used to run together back in what I called the "Viking days," leading armies on horseback, burning entire cities to the ground.

He was **YETAREL**, who outranked Azazel, but had renounced his rank for reasons known only to himself. His father was motherfucking Lucifer. Ours would be a Royal wedding.

138

Needless to say, Azazel was pissed. He tormented me relentlessly in my dreams, waking me up every night at exactly 3:33 to taunt me, and often my parked truck would rock back and forth as I heard loud bangs like pounding... but when I parted the curtains to look outside no-one was ever there.

There were an unusual number of near misses as cars inexplicably veered into my path two or three times a day. I was stressed the fuck out and losing a lot of sleep.

I began praying to Lucifer regularly to keep me safe, but he never answered. Clint told me Lucifer was very busy with other things. He formally introduced me to PAIMON and told me he would send something to keep me safe. He called it "The Dragon." Surprisingly, the number of cars randomly veering into my path dropped down to zero, as if something was scaring them away.

One night, driving through construction in heavy rain, into oncoming traffic with no divider except a row of orange plastic "donkey dick" pylons, listening to an album on *Spotify*, a song from a completely different album began playing: "Psychopomp" by *The Tea Party,* and an intense image of Azazel's face suddenly lunged out of the darkness into my windshield, nearly wrecking my truck. I could see nothing but that angry face. This was immediately followed by a blinding flash of light and something else manifested directly behind him. A man, dressed in a white suit, lounging upon a white throne, with one leg across his knee and his elbow on the arm of the throne with his chin resting upon his fist, completely relaxed and at ease. He looked like Clint, but older with shockingly white hair. Lucifer was nothing like I'd ever imagined him to be... he was gangsta as fuck... and he just kicked Azazel's ass with nothing more than a *thought*. A moment later, both of them were gone and I could see the road again.

That one fleeting instant changed my outlook on everything. I had respected and admired Lucifer all my life, but I had always thought of him as darker, a destructive force, but he wasn't dark at all... he was like white phosphorous. Lucifer himself just intervened on my behalf, like the brightest and most powerful guardian angel of all, the Lord of Light, the Morning Star. After all those years of working with the Dark Ones, I finally knew where I stood and whose side I was on.

139

The wedding was to take place on 6-6-16... which turned out to be a Monday, so instead we planned it on Sunday evening with the reception carrying over until the next day. It was to be at *Church* nightclub, a deconsecrated Lutheran church over a century old which was my home away from home... I went there every Sunday night for decades and was friends with the managers, bartenders, DJs, and security... still, it would cost us over a thousand dollars to rent the venue for the two hours before it opened to the public.

We did not have much money, so I posted my first and only *Kickstarter* fundraiser a month before our wedding, thinking that if a hundred of our friends each donated only ten bucks we'd be covered, and figured it wouldn't take that long at all. People donated what they could, but we were still short. The final week, a few of Clint's friends... mostly people he only knew online and had never actually met... donated the remainder of what we needed.

We decided to keep the guest list very small, because we would be performing a high level magickal rite and needed to filter unstable or antagonistic energies.

In addition to renting *Church*, we needed to buy my wedding dress, the cake, catering, a case of champagne, and a handle of *Black Magic* rum. I got a great deal on my dress because I provided the material and the design... the seamstress was my best friend's boss and owner of *The Secret Boutique* who only charged me $1,500 for putting my vision together, in exchange for giving her full rights to the pattern... it was emerald green with black lace and looked like something out of a fairy tale... and instead of a veil, I opted for a mask... a gold 13 point star with a face. My friend who took me to *Disguises* exclaimed, *"That looks like the Morning Star!"* Exactly.

We sent out 55 invitations and got only 30 RVSPs, 10 of which were people Clint had invited. The energy for this rite needed to be perfect. We couldn't have a heckler or spaz showing up. Hence, stipulations engraved upon the invitations read:

1. Once the doors close at 7 PM, they will not reopen again under any circumstances, whether to let people in or out.
2. If your name is not on the List as an invited guest or +1, you are not getting past the door.
3. Absolutely no-one wearing anything orange will be admitted under any circumstances.

The "orange" thing was almost an afterthought, but Clint insisted it was important because our color scheme was Green & Black and orange was Azazel's favorite color. Only a few people asked about it and were told simply, "It's an Irish thing."

Clint bought a bunch of things off eBay with which to assemble the cake topper himself. It was a representation of us in our angelic aspects, as YETAREL with his golden armor and flaming sword, and UZAZIEL with her sickle and jeweled goblet... they stood in a grassy field with a Rottweiler puppy at their feet. It was perfect in every way, and serves as our altar piece today.

140

Our wedding day was a shitstorm of epic proportions.

First, on his way to the caterer, Clint was nearly T-boned by an unmarked garbage truck that ran a red light in Cap Hill at nearly double the speed limit. Every garbage truck in town has a business name, phone number, and DOT number clearly painted on the side... this had none of that and it was a near miss. If he hadn't tapped the brakes to check an incoming text it would've slammed right through his Toyota. This was no accident... this was practically a guided missile.

Next, when we arrived at *Church* at 6 PM as scheduled, all the doors were locked, no-one was there, and none of the managers were answering their phones. The buttercream icing on the cake was starting to melt in the 90 degree heat and guests began arriving early.

The doors finally opened at 6:20, giving us only 40 minutes to set up... and it was 110 degrees inside because the air conditioning was broken. The staff put the three tier cake in the beer cooler. It was chocolate with raspberry filling and emerald green icing.

Eric helped to hang the 4 foot by 4 inch tubular chime, which weighed about thirty pounds and provided the most resonant bass note, which I felt was far superior to any bell or gong. That particular note was the most important element of the rite... that tone was the key to a very specific portal.

Clint prepared the ritual space while Jewelz helped with my dress. It was rather elaborate with a hoop skirt and laced corset which required a lot of help. The heat was so bad poor Jewelz actually fainted and needed to be revived and taken outside while I struggled along myself as best I could.

We were expecting trouble, so Clint took no chances. In addition to the club's entire security staff being there, the President of a local motorcycle club was working the door and Clint had prearranged for two people to help him out during the ceremony: the Ogre and the Imp.

The Ogre was his stepson who had driven here from New York. He looked like an enforcer from the Chinese mob, but was actually a supervising investigator for Child Protective Services... didn't make him any less scary though. Clint reached into a backpack and handed him a gigantic spontoon fighting pick... basically a medieval battle axe with a sharpened spike instead of an edge, and said, "If anyone intrudes upon the ceremony after those doors are closed, put this through their fucking chest." Everyone in the audience went pale. "Alright," the Ogre said, and returned to his seat.

The Imp was a tiny Asian girl who was legitimately psychotic and found distinguishing between reality and fantasy challenging. She had been my "club daughter" for years and was fanatically loyal to me. He handed her a heavy rubber cat o' nine tails flogger that could easily tear flesh. "If anyone here dares to disrupt the ceremony, hit them across the face with this as hard as you can." There was a collective gasp. "Yesssssss..." she said, then began giggling.

I had intended to carry a black metal censer, swinging from a chain, filled with burning charcoal and frankincense, in lieu of a bouquet, for my walk down the aisle. Everything was perfect and ready to go, when suddenly I felt a presence, saw an orange spark zip past, heard laughter in my ear, and the censer which had been completely stable and motionless suddenly upended and dumped red hot coals down the front of my dress!

Miraculously, neither myself nor the dress were burned. Somehow, it wasn't even stained with soot. That silk was not fire resistant and very easily could've gone up in flames, immolating me. A photograph of me taken moments later clearly showed three bright orange streaks in close formation just behind my head. The Enemy was trying everything he could to stop this ceremony from happening!

After a fifteen minute delay, which caused the DJ to begin playing music early to calm the audience in the sweltering heat, I put on my mask and began walking down the aisle, unexpectedly and way off cue. "King of the World" by *Chthonic Force* was supposed to have been my wedding march... I don't know what the fuck was playing but it wasn't that.

Jett was supposed to be officiating, and there were about twenty lines he was supposed to read *before* the wedding march began, but that didn't happen either... he looked confused and scared, as did Ajay our DJ. Clint's eyes got huge. He knew something had gone terribly wrong.

He drew the blackjack from his pocket and spun around, striking the tubular bell as hard as he could, filling the *Church* with a tone so loud the windows shook, then he drew his athame and carved the sigil of Lucifer in the ether.

I was scared and upset... nothing was going according to plan! Then he turned back to me and took my hand, looking me in the eyes, and I knew everything was fine and nothing else mattered.

Much later, he told me that he saw my lips say, *"It's okay,"* and thought I was wearing gold makeup and lipstick under my mask, but I was wearing a full face mask and I did not say any such thing. After examining the mask he swore he saw my lips and jaw moving, stating that this was a clear case of "overshadowing" in which a spirit partially manifests as an illusory mask over one's face... or, in this case, a mask over a mask.

He hugged me close, whispering in my ear, *"Fuck all these people... this is just for us,"* whereupon I laughed, reassured that everything was exactly as it should be. Then he drew the other knife... a long hooked blade with a needle sharp tip that he'd had custom made by one of his friends in Paris specifically for this ceremony. We each pricked our thumbs and signed the contract in blood. **"Bound for life,"** he said.

"Bound in blood," I replied.

He turned towards the audience, most of whom were meeting him for the very first time, holding the aged parchment high and yelled:

"IN NOMINUS LUCIFER!

I HEREBY CONSECRATE THIS TEMPLE AND SANCTIFY THIS UNION!

BEHOLD HIS SIGN AND SEAL!

MORTUUS TYRANNIS!!!"

The contract fucking supernovaed... it didn't merely burst into flame, it lit up the room like a magnesium flare for nearly a full minute before it fell to the floor as ash. Somehow, Clint was unburned. It was a neat trick... 4 sheets of nitrocellulose flash paper had been glued to the back of the teastained onionskin contract, then ignited with a magician's device concealed in his palm. The glue and layering slowed the burn rate considerably so it blazed instead of popped.

Everyone in the room sat there in shock, unsure of what they'd just witnessed. *"The Rite of Blood and Flame"* was intended to be over a half hour long and we had compressed and condensed it into about three minutes. To say it was "intense" would be an understatement.

Jett was off to the side, high as fuck and completely lost... which was quite understandable as none of this was on his script. We had him read his lines, then we exchanged our formal vows, sipped some 50 year old Port from a chalice, and signed the official Marriage License. Everyone clapped.

The staff brought the cake downstairs because it was at least 30 degrees cooler there and everyone was sweating through their fancy clothes and half dead from heat exhaustion.

The doorman approached Clint and told him that moments before the door was sealed at 7 PM a late arrival stated he was "here for the wedding" but refused to give his name, becoming hostile and belligerent when he was told there was a List.

He was described as a big muscular skinhead guy wearing combat boots, black military style cargo pants, and an "obnoxiously bright orange T-shirt, like something a hunter would wear." The doorman remembered the "no orange rule" so that really made him take notice. He told the guy he'd be right back, then locked him outside.

Neither of us had any idea who this could've been. This was especially significant to me because the night before, at the usual time of 3:33, I awoke from a nightmare about a stranger with a shaved head barging into our wedding and shooting Clint dead just before we exchanged our vows.

Everything changed after that ritual. It was like a huge weight had suddenly been lifted from me. It took hours before I finally realized the enormity of what had occurred... the thick black tendril connecting me to Azazel had been severed.

I was free.

Epilogue

After the wedding, several of my friends approached Clint to shake his hook and thank him for marrying me. "You have no idea how angry and sad she always was, I've known Queen for twenty years and have never seen her so happy" was the gist of what most of them said.

Later that night, we were surprised to see a thick swirling mist throughout the Dark Room... they never run a fog machine in this venue... but it was not fog. It was not smoke. It was not steam. It was *spirits*... hundreds of them... briefly manifested to bear witness and pay their respects. No-one saw them but us, and an hour later they were gone.

Exactly one year later, on our Anniversary, I discovered the long lost Celtic knotwork ring I used to wear on the streets which was nearly an exact match to my wedding band. It was in an old box I'd had in storage and had already gone through several times... I am positive it was not in that box before. Somehow, the spirits discovered my lost ring and apported it into a box I was opening on our Anniversary day. Clint has been wearing it ever since.

There are a lot of things that were not covered in this book. Several relationships and jobs were omitted entirely. Most of my spiritual experiences occurred on the Astral, which is very difficult to convey as the descriptions sound almost indistinguishable from extremely vivid lucid dreams. Many other experiences were extremely subtle, like a feeling, a coincidence, a brief flash of a vision.

Azazel's influence over others is difficult to describe. Rarely would it be a full possession by him personally... often a subordinate would take possession... but I would always *smell* him, for want of a better word. You know how you get a whiff of ozone and feel waves of static electricity when you are standing next to a high voltage transformer humming with power? It is sort of like that, and his Name would suddenly flash into my mind, or sometimes an image of his face. The possessed person would invariably display certain mannerisms, such as that distinct *smirk*, as well as demonstrate a high level of psychic ability, revealing that which was hidden or invading a dream. Often, electrical devices would be affected: streetlights would burn out, cars or computers would inexplicably malfunction, or a song I did not even have in my collection would begin playing in the middle of one of my *Spotify* playlists, like "Rainbow in the Dark" by *DIO*, the lyrics of which were a clear threat. "Psychopomp" by *The Tea Party* is another favorite of his. Those songs have come on prior to him manifesting on several occasions. He has a huge ego and enjoys being dramatic like that.

Some things are nearly impossible to convey. Several times a Fallen manifested in our darkened bedroom and was observed via clairvoyant sight. This is a 5th or 6th dimensional being we are looking at on the 4th dimension through our closed eyelids... it appears as nothing one can describe in words. Words are inadequate. One manifestation appeared as a black Christmas tree composed of paisley designs moving like clockwork while multicolored beams of light flashed in every direction. Ezekiel's description of "wheels within wheels" makes a little more sense now. We are incapable of perceiving their true form, but merely an approximation of an incomplete segment protruding into our reality.

I understand that few people will believe these words. "Lies and delusions!" they shall accuse. Behold all the fucks I give about what you think. All my life I have been called "Crazy Queen" by the normies, my exes, even my own mother. You are not expected to believe me. This book was not written for you. I wrote this book as my sole Legacy... a recording of a life... a scream into the Void. After I'm dead, this book will be the only evidence I ever existed at all. If you expect "proof" of angels and demons, good luck with that, people have been trying to prove that for thousands of years.

After our wedding, Lucifer forbade Azazel from directly engaging me, so instead he sent others on his behalf: Asmodai, the Dark Ones, *djinn*. We have both been subject to regular psychic attacks and malicious manifestations for years, which are ongoing. Lots of bad luck involving circumstances beyond our control, random strangers targeting us, being viciously attacked in our dreams. I came off the road to take a local job once I was married, and this whirlwind of spiritual animosity, which only affected my dear husband during the weekend I visited once a month, now became a daily part of his life.

Next came visits from a group of entities I call the "Gumshoes" because they always appeared dressed as old fashioned private eyes from the 1940s with the tan trenchcoats and fedoras. They were obviously high ranking neutral parties tasked with investigating some sort of unspecified grievance against me. I do not believe this grievance was filed by Azazel, but by the Dark Ones I worked with in my youth, who became enraged after my wedding, claiming I had betrayed them by "turning Light." Let me tell you this, tentacle rape on the Astral isn't nearly as enjoyable as those *hentai* cartoons make it seem... I always thought of them as friends and Brethren, but they turned on me viciously and without mercy. Those visitations were fairly regular for a couple of months, the Gumshoes politely asking me a series of questions which I answered honestly and openly in full detail, before the visits abruptly stopped. This was nothing like the MIB phenomenon but something completely different which we can find no reference to in any occult text. I do not know who the Gumshoes were, but got the impression they were unbiased and fair.

A cult devoted to AZAZEL formed in neighboring Boulder, and a seer we know had a series of visions about them and was threatened on the Astral by a demon stating he was "coming for Queen." A streetrat I knew for many years was taken in by them, possessed, and began stalking me both on social media and at the club. All of my evil exes inexplicably reappeared in the Denver scene at the same time. Then a series of crazed strangers began randomly targeting us whenever we were in town.

This culminated when a new arrival in Denver began relentlessly stalking me, a biker who knew my old friend Gimp and became immersed in the local outlaw motorcycle clubs, trying to stir up drama and spread false rumors to cause trouble. Clairvoyant observation by myself and several others revealed him to be possessed by a high ranking subordinate of ASMODAI. He legitimately threatened to kidnap me and after his one attempt was foiled, I was poisoned while dancing with my burlesque family at *3 Kings*. An associate of his in another club dosed my rum with methanol fuel additive which sent me to the ER and nearly killed me. Clint handled that by talking to some of the baddest bikers in the state, who basically told "Slenderman" he wasn't allowed in Denver anymore and he disappeared shortly thereafter.

Asmodai and the *djinn* sent several more "skin suits" into my clubs to physically threaten or attack me, including another guy like Jonathan who liked to show off with the blue flaming aura trick. Several of my close friends have also been targeted for harassment, stalking, threats... including one girl who was kidnapped from the club and raped.

Every time we return to Denver shit immediately starts up again. Denver is the focal point, a giant swirling vortex. It is extremely dangerous for me there, but *Church, Milkbar,* and *3 Kings* are within my Domain where I have held Court for years and *nothing* will ever frighten me away from my Home... that is non-fucking-negotiable.

There is a strong possibility I may be killed soon. Forces have aligned against us. As powerful as we might be, with a contingent of formidable spirits as allies, the Enemy is constantly watching, biding his time, lying in wait. You need to understand that "time" is meaningless to them... a year passes like a second and they have minions who exist only to lurk... they have all the time in the world, and they only need to get lucky once.

I would be lying if I said I wasn't scared... but there are far worse things than being scared: cowardice, dishonor, apathy. I refuse to run or hide. I will face my fears, with my beloved at my side, zero fucks given.

I have found my true love. We declare loyalty to LUCIFER and are aligned "Chaotic Neutral." We did not start this quarrel, so if we are attacked know that we were acting on behalf of the Light, however shit goes down. We just want to be left alone, but understand Azazel will never give up.

We shall die on our feet, together, fighting to the very end. *So it is written, so shall it be done.*

Printed in Great Britain
by Amazon

16856706R00192